Outer Wilds Complete Guide

Kade Veum

ISBN: 979-8-3528-8992-3

ISBN: 979-8-3528-8992-3

CONTENTS

Forge

Echoes of the Eye DLC

You're the newest member of Outer Wilds Ventures, a fledgling space program searching for answers in a strange, constantly changing solar system. Who built the ruins on the moon? What lurks in the heart of Dark Bramble? Why are you trapped in a time loop, and can it be stopped? To solve these mysteries you'll have to venture into the most dangerous reaches of space.

Strap on your hiking boots, check your oxygen levels, and get ready to venture into space. Use the Little Scout space probe to illuminate dark caves, take photos, or test for hazards in your environment. Track down mysterious audio with your Signal Scope or use your Translator to decipher an ancient Nomai riddle. Navigate the darkness of space with your jetpack and ship. There's a lot to discover in the Outer Wilds.

Our guides will walk you through every step of the way, using the clues you gather at each location to point your way to the next. We'll start on Timber Hearth's moon, the Attlerock, and follow the clues from there to the game's other planets, like Brittle Hollow and Giant's Deep.

INTRODUCTION

Welcome to the Outer Wilds wiki guide. In this guide we will be helping you solve puzzles within the game and uncover all the secrets and oddities within it. This page contains the introduction area to the game and the initial systems it teaches.

Waking Up

Upon starting the game you'll wake up on your home planet of Timber Hearth in Hearthian village, looking up at the stars with a crackling campfire nearby. You'll have the fun option of roasting marshmallows on this fire if you so choose.

Nearby you can talk to a fellow Hearthian named Slate, who informs you that you are an astronaut for the clan, and that today is your Launch Day. He let's you know that you'll need to get launch codes from Hornfels at the observatory before you can lift off and to bring them back here where the docking bay is once you've finished in the area.

Think of this initial area as a tutorial to get acquainted with some of the controls and systems of the game. There's a handful of people to talk to but we'll highlight the ones that help teach you some vital knowledge.

Model Ship Flight Simulation

First up is controls with a toy model ship, after jumping up a series of rocks (press and hold A, then release to jump), you'll find a model shop docked on an outcrop overlooking the village. Interact with this ship to get a sense of how flight is going to work in the game.

Flight can get quite tricky and you'll need to be careful not to crash into things (lest you wish to be continuously repairing your ship). While easier to do in first person once on the ship this model toy example teaches how there's up and down thrust as well as a horizontal thrust. Use the left stick to move on the horizontal plane (forward, back, and side to side) and the triggers to control your verticality (up and down). Play around with this a bit to get a feel for how this works. It becomes even more challenging in zero gravity, but we'll get there in a moment.

Instruments and Using Signalscope

Speaking with the Hearthian playing the banjo named Gneiss, you'll find that there are several space explorers on other planets using various instruments that she made. There's Chert and his drums, Riebeck using a banjo, Gabbro with a flute, and Feldspar using a harmonica, though she informs you that Feldspar's been missing for awhile.

To find these musicians you can used your Signalscope out in space to track down the sound of their instruments. How does one do this? Well thankfully we have Tephra and Galena to teach us using a quick game of hide and seek. Speak to them, and they'll initiate a game of hide and seek where you'll use your Signalscope to find them using the radios they hold.

To use your Signalscope press Y and it will bring up a strange instrument in your first person view with two half rings. As you aim in different directions you may notice these rings coming together and glowing green. This indicates the direction of a point of interest. Walk in that direction to find it.

Keep in mind that it will point towards DIRECTLY where the noise is, not in the direction of where you need to got to get to that point.

You'll find Tephra on a rock outcrop behind a waterfall:

While Galena can be found hiding behind some barrels you'll have to jump across a ramped building to reach:

Ghost Matter

Further up the path on the way to the observatory, you'll find a sectioned off area with a note in front of it explaining that contained ahead is a section of Ghost Matter, a freezing cold and invisible substance that will burn you as you walk through it.

If you walk to the right to the nearby camera and look through it, you'll easily see a cloud of green energy in the snapshots you take. Keep this in mind later as you explore.

Zero-G Flight

To the right of the fenced off Ghost Matter, you'll find a cave with a sign next to it that reads "Zero-G Cave." Inside you'll find a Hearthian named Gossan who claims there's a "satellite" in need of repairs in the zero-g cave (it's really broken mining equipment), and asks if you'd be willing to go fix it. While this seems like a distraction from your main task, this area will teach you about flying in Zero Gravity, so it's a good idea to at least try it out.

Head to the lift and activate it sending you deep underground. Down here it will be super dark. Click in your right analog stick to see with your flashlight.

Head through the archway to where you'll com to a wall with a suit hung on it. Press X to put on the suit.

This suit's controls work exactly like flying the model ship earlier, only now you'll be in first person making it a bit easier to control.

Go up using RT to scale the wall, and land on a small platform. Ahead you'll find a massive drop off. Head on down, but be careful to use your upward thrust to soften the gravitational fall. Next head into the pit up ahead, where now you'll be in Zero Gravity. Down here you'll need to position yourself in front of 3 separate repair points on the mining equipment. After positioning yourself you can lock on to the broken area by pressing in the Left analog stick and then repair it with X.

Make sure to keep an eye on your fuel gauge in the top left corner, and note the oxygen gauge as well, something that will come into play later.

Note that while in flight in Zero Gravity, you can use A to stabilize yourself to whatever speed the object you're trying to reach is going. This can be extremely helpful once planets are in orbit and moving around the sun in space.

After repairing all three break points, use your remain gin fuel to thrust yourself upward out of the Zero-G Cave. Then, replace the suit back on the wall and head on out and up towards the observatory.

The Observatory

After leaving the Zero-G Cave, head left toward the Observatory. Once inside, first you'll see a large statue of a strange head and a Hearthian named Hal standing near it. He informs you that its a representation of a race called the Nomai, and until now Hearthians hadn't known about the Nomai having fur.

This race's trace artifacts left on many of the planets will be some of the most mysterious parts of the game.

Head to the right into the observatory and up the central spiral to find Hornfels in front of a computer. Speaking with him, he informs you that in addition to your first voyage, this is also the first voyage being done with the added use of a Nomai translator tool, allowing you to decipher scrawling of the mysterious race left on the different planets. When prompted that you're ready, he'll give you the launch codes to the ship and you can be on your way.

However, not so fast. As you exit the observatory and pass the strange statue, it turns to look at you and its eyes open, showing a vision of everything you've done thus far. Creepy.

Make your way down to the launch area and you can use them on the elevator to reach your ship, and make your way into the vast explorable distance beyond!

One More Thing...

One more quick thing of note. Eventually as you journey through space, you're going to die. Inevitably from either the sun exploding (as we find out shortly is inevitable) or from your own initial mishaps of a first time explorer. Strangeness is afoot, as when you die your progress is reviewed by some strange beings (probably the Nomai given the process is similar to the event in the Observatory), and you're sent back to the starting point of the game, only you keep any progress you've gained, but you'll always wake up once again near the campfire, and head out from this point. Got it? Good! NOW GO EXPLORE!

SUN STATION

The Sun Station was a location built by the Nomai to harness the power of an exploding sun and use it within time warping. However getting there to see for yourself its secrets can be a little tricky. Here's how to do it.

How to Arrive at Sun Station

If you've explored a good amount of Outer Wilds, you probably know by now that the Nomai used teleportation to whip around this solar system using Black Holes created in the Black Hole Forge. Likewise, from spending time on Ash Twin, we know that this became a hub of sorts for all the transportation to all the planets within the solar system.

Now, you may be able to see the Sun Station from space at different times, however, landing on it is next to impossible. Instead we're going to use Ash Twin's teleportation for it.

Head to Ash Twin and park at one of the poles to avoid your ship being swept up by the large column of shifting sands that circles the planet.

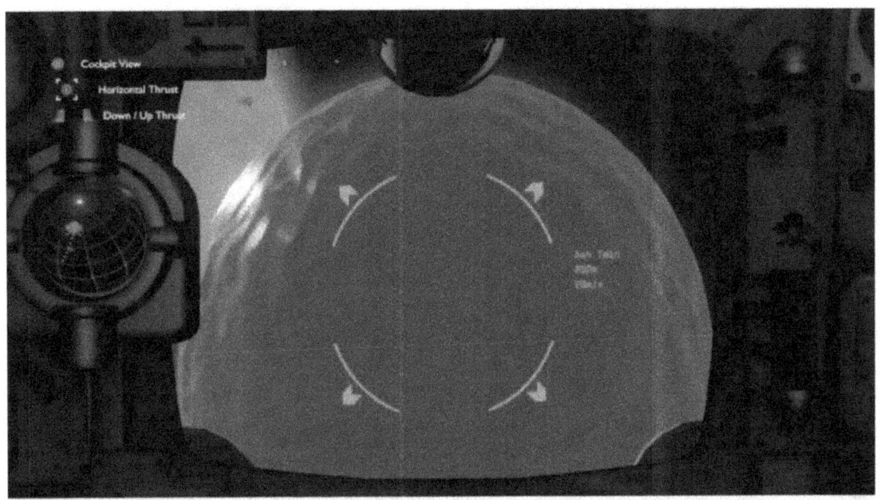

As the sand is picked up, the first building to be revealed, along with the first location you can teleport to, is the sun shaped building teleporting you to the Sun Station.

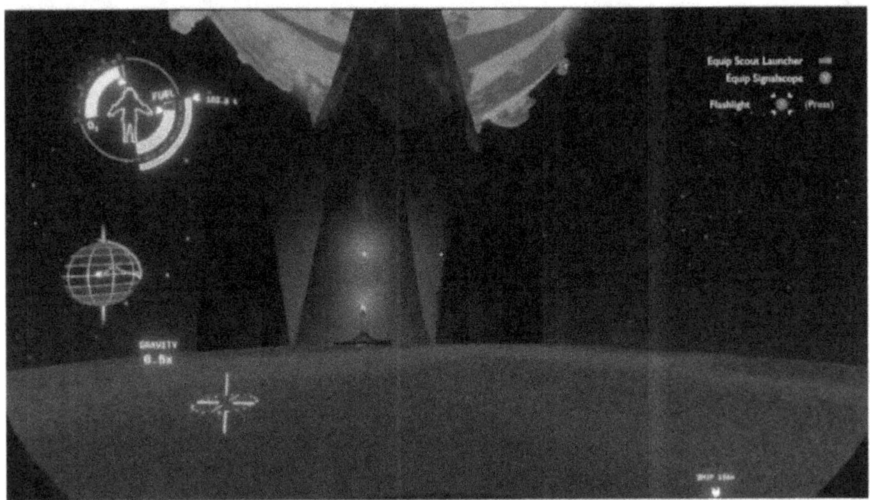

Wait until the sands have moved below the entrance and then quickly make your way in. You'll need to use the sinking sands to your advantage, avoiding hazardous cacti as you make your way inside, then right, and following the path, you'll arrive at a transporter beam that will move you upwards into a large room.

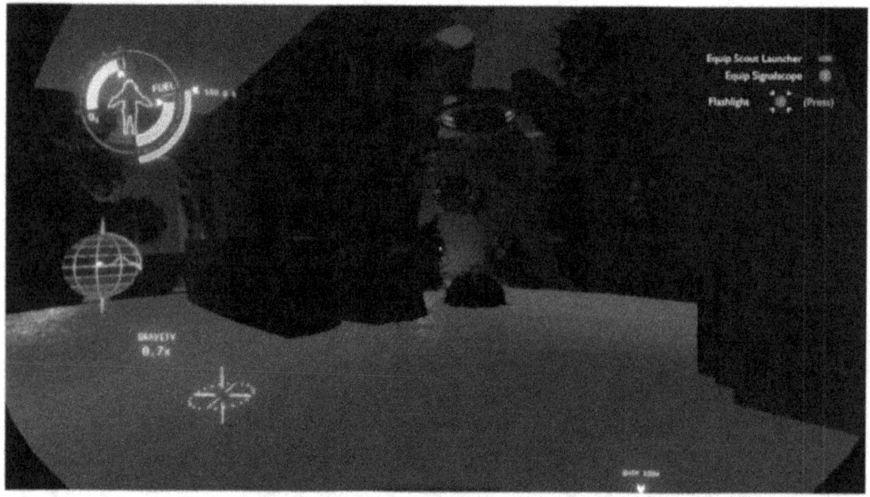

If you've used a Black Hole Teleporter before in the game, you'll know that the large pane of glass in the center of the room on the floor is this device, and that you'll need to stand on it and look for the destination to pass you (in this case, look up), then you'll teleport to it.

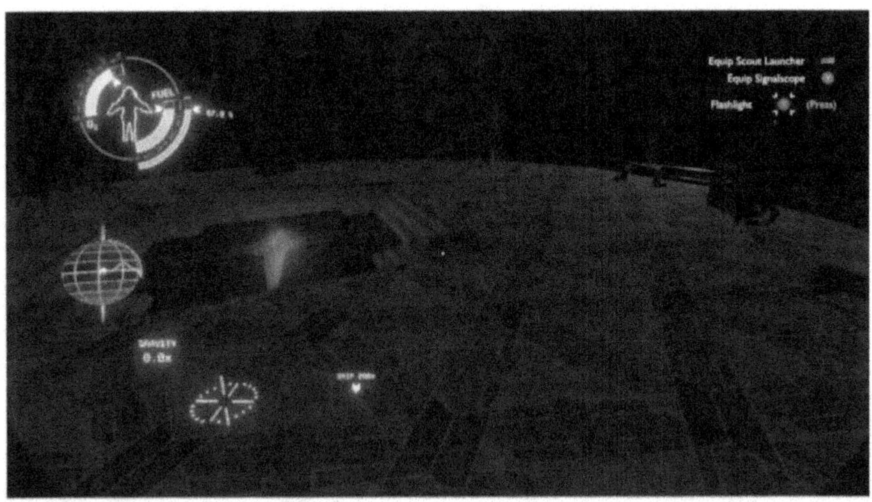

Once you've teleported, you should find yourself in a large room stuck to a gravity floor. Go down the wall ahead of you, and then onto the floor. Nearby will be a door you can open up to reveal a large gap you'll have to cross using your jets.

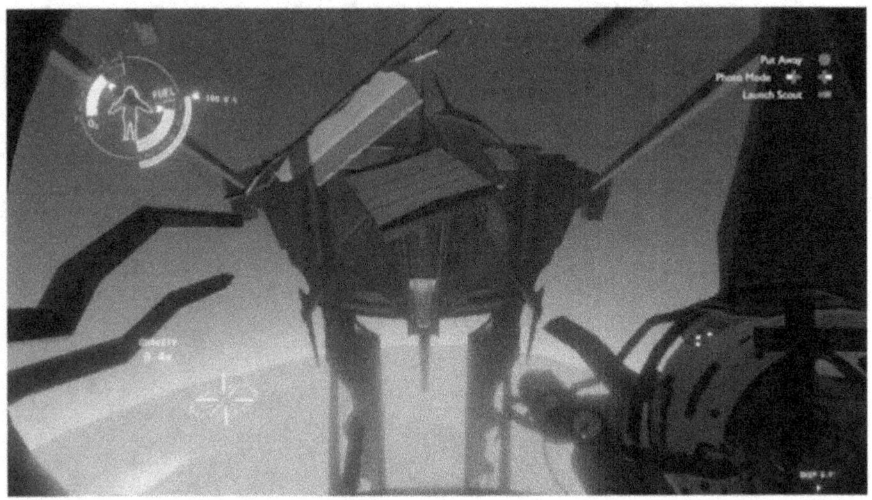

Thankfully, it's zero G so just boost out to the doorway across the gap and carefully maneuver yourself inside.

The Secrets of the Sun Station

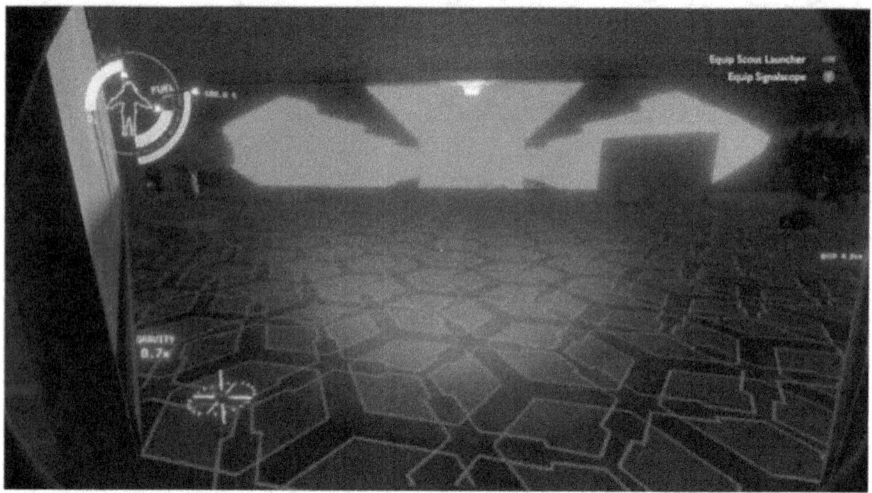

Inside you learn that the purpose of this station was to cause the sun of this solar system to go supernova, hypothetically creating the energy needed for the time interval experiment and to launch the Orbital Probe. However, as we learn from translation, the experiment failed.

EMBER TWIN

The Ember Twin is one of the two Hourglass Twins, two small planets orbiting one another that are closest to the sun. Below you'll find the different activities and puzzles found on the Ember Twin.

Chert's Camp

At the North Pole of the Ember Twin you'll find a drum playing NPC named Chert. He informs you that the stars are all dying! WHAT!?

He's gone completely mental in reaction to this news about your own stars imminent death and doesn't seem too interested in anything you have to say.

The Mysterious Teleporting Rock

If you happen to pull out your signal scope and search for Quantum frequencies while on Ember Twin, you may find several caves with a strange rock in them that will vanish whenever you're not looking.

You'll find one of the caves south of Chert's camp and the north pole. you'll find it based on the large pillars holding up the entrance.

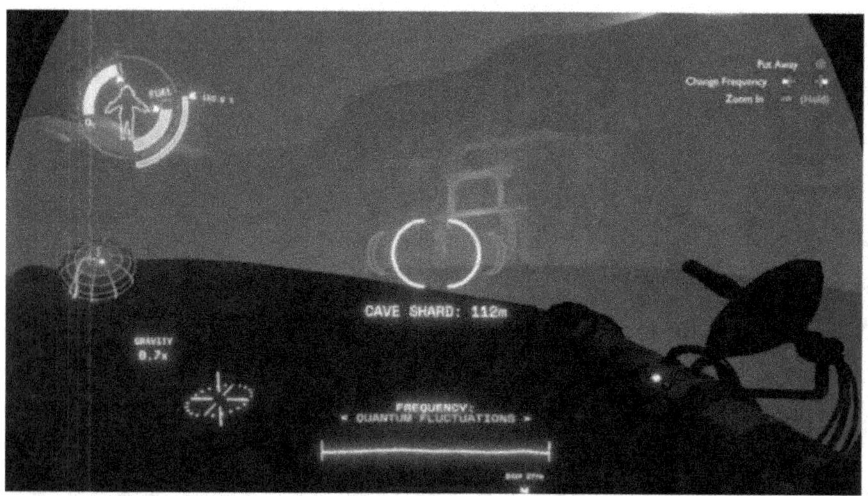

Heading in you'll find a text on the wall detailing how one of the Nomai disappeared while researching the rock. It also mentions that he initially vanished in a dry Lakebed Cave.

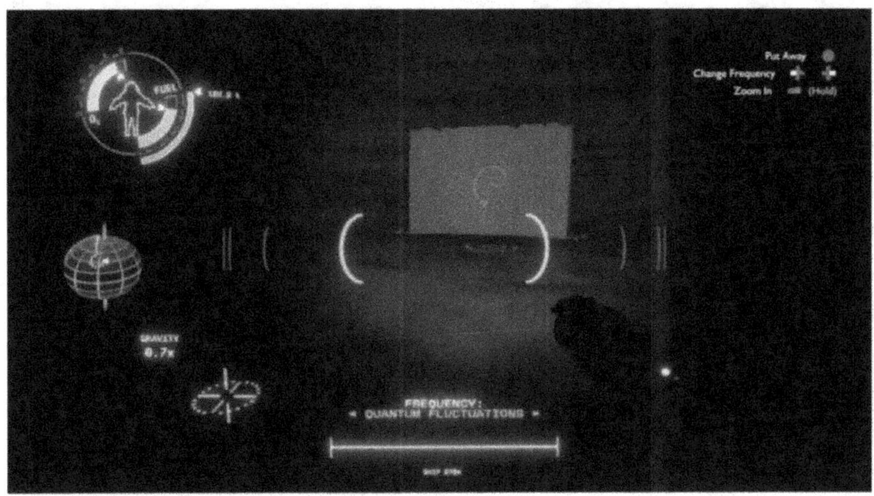

You'll find another cave with a stack of three pillars holding up the entrance on the opposite side of Chert's Camp. Inside, you'll find more notes from the geology expedition. A note on the floor once again informs you of the vanishing Nomai, and a note on the wall details the finding of the rock and how it wanders like the Quantum Moon does, but you already knew that.

We'll need to reach this Lakebed Cave to find out more, so let's head there.

Getting to the Lakebed Cave

Actually getting to the Lakebed Cave proves to be quite the challenge especially with the rising sands.

First, head to the lakebed beneath Chert's camp. It's a long way down, so use your boosters at the base to avoid damage. Once at the bottom continue further into the earth.

Continue following the path. You may find your way blocked by stalactites and stalagmites, just follow the open area. Eventually you should arrive at a wall of sand falling down. Head through this.

Falling down you'll come into a room with more blockades, both rock and cactus. These actually behave as quantum objects, meaning if you continue to look away and then look at where they were, eventually they'll disappear, clearing a path.

Continue deeper, using your knowledge of quantum objects to move blockages in your way. Eventually you'll come to a cave with the strange rock, and some notes on the ground.

They relay that while they've come to visit the cave to find the missing Nomai, he isn't here. The notes relay how the events took place. The now missing Nomai had been standing on the rock when the lights went out, and when they returned on, both he and the rock were gone. (wink wink nudge nudge)

Learning the Second Rule

Armed with this knowledge, we can now solve the mystery of the teleporting rock and missing Nomai. As mentioned in the note, we'll need to turn off the lights via a switch nearby. Keep your flashlight on though.

Climb on top of the rock with your flashlight aimed at the rock, and then flick it off and then back on.

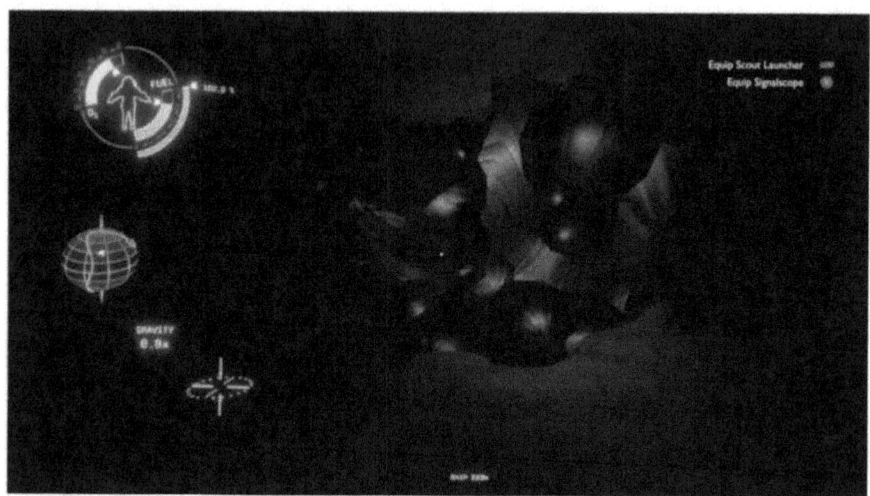

You'll teleport with the rock and find yourself in a new room. This is the room the missing Nomai had traveled to as evidenced by the nearby writing on the wall. The Nomai noticed this new room has no entrance or exit to it, and the rock teleported without him looking at it. He experiments with the rock and discovers a new quantum rule:

If in contact with a quantum object and in total darkness, you will travel with that quantum object.

The Sunless City

A city left behind in the depths of Ember Twin, getting there can be tricky enough, although inside there are plenty of secrets to uncover.

Getting to the Sunless City

To get to the Sunless City, first head for the distress beacon left by the 2nd of the 3 escape pods on the surface of Ember Twin. You'll see it from space by the large glowing blue beam of light.

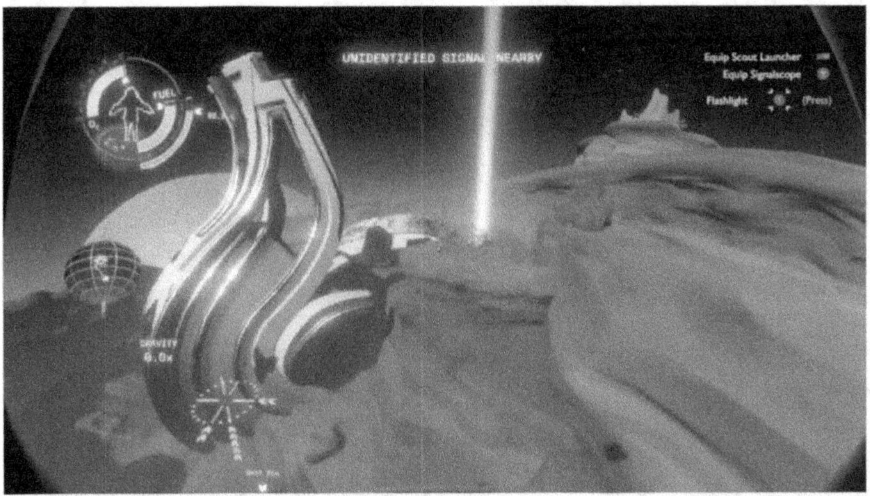

Land and follow the cable into the ship where you can translate a few Nomai recordings to learn of a crash that many survived. Head out the back of the ship via the escape hatch, using your cursor to move the glowing ball to unlock the door.

You'll find yourself in a large underground passage. On the walls the Nomai left writings for their comrades to be able to find them as they made their way deeper beneath the earth.

Follow the clues as they lead you through the winding tunnels, especially once they mention to follow the instructions closely to avoid getting lost. Here they all are so there's no need to write them down yourself:

Walk forward until you meet the sandfall at the pit and turn left

continue to the room filled with rock column formations and climb upward through the opening above them

Continue to follow the path until you come to another set of writings.

Make the leap across the now broken bridge.

Head through the sand column.

Continue to follow the path until you reach another note telling you to hurry due to the falling sand.

Jump the gap up to another sand column you'll walk through to find yourself in front of the door to the Sunless City.

Up the stairs to your left you'll find a viewpoint for an Angler Fish fossil that gives a vital clue in relation to Dark Bramble. But more on that in a moment.

Go ahead and open the door to the city and head on in. We'll go over the important things to keep in mind there.

Navigating the Sunless City

As you enter you'll find yourself in a vast cavern. To your right you should see a large glowing light illuminating an area with trees and four column switches.

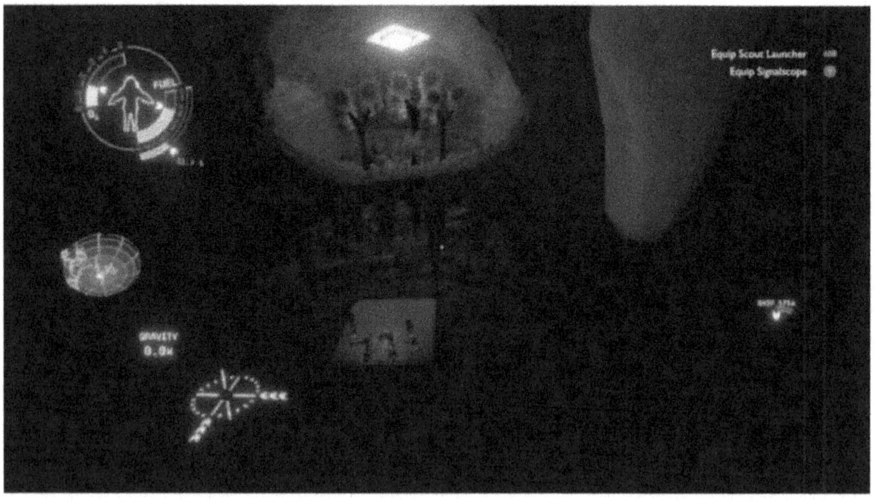

Fly over there to refill your oxygen tank, then take a look at the wall nearby. Via translation there, you learn of a proposed Sun Station that was necessary for the completion of the Ash Twin Project, the Sun Station will be a section in and of itself. If you wish to learn how to get there, head on over to the Sun Station Page.

Now let's take a look at those column switches behind you. Each illuminates an area of the Sunless City that acts as a pathway to the area it denotes on the stone beneath it.

From left to right you have:

Anglerfish Overlook District

Stepping Stone District

High Energy Lab Trailhead

Eye Shrine District

Explore all four to learn all the secrets they hold, but the two of note we'll focus on are the High Energy Lab and the Anglerfish Overlook/Stepping Stone District.

A Quick Shortcut: If you take the path to the Gravity Cannon, you'll find a small hole in the side of the wall surrounding the Cannon that you can easily use for future entry into the Sunless City without the hassle of retracing your earlier steps through the caves.

Learning the Anglerfish Secret

To learn the crucial secret of getting past the Anglerfish in Dark Bramble, we'll need to study the fossil hidden within the Sunless City.

To do so, we'll have to follow the instructions of a game Nomai children seemed to play with this fossil long ago.

Remember the Anglerfish Overlook you passed earlier? Well as denoted by the translations found within the Sunless City, the first step to this game is to throw a lantern down into its mouth. For you your "lantern" is of course your Scout. So step 1: head back to the Overlook and fire your Scout into the Anglerfish Fossil's maw.

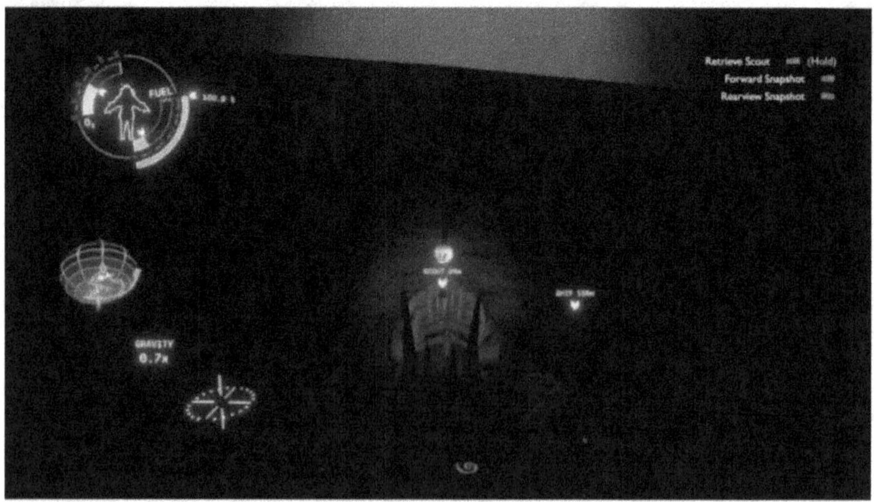

Via another set of writings from the children, we also know that once you've thrown your "lantern" into the mouth of the fossil, head to the Stepping Stone District for the Fossil to "show you the way."

Use the light switches near the trees to find the Stepping Stone District and head there, then follow through the caves until you look up and see the light shining inside the top of the Anglerfish Mouth. From here you can easily boost up into the mouth.

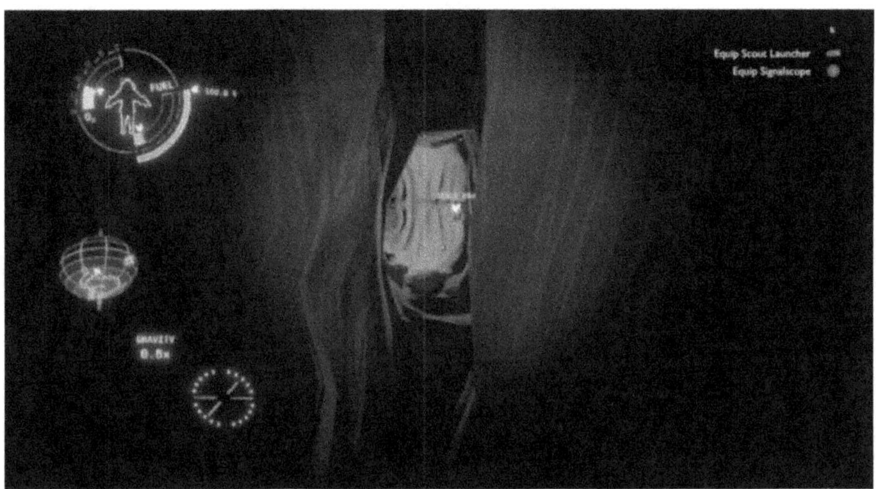

Nearby the Fossil on the ground you'll find writings giving you a crucial clue in relation to live Anglerfish:

Anglerfish are blind, and can only attack what they hear.

High Energy Lab

From the light switches in the Sunless City, select the one for the High Energy Lab Trailhead to reveal a stairway at the base of the Sunless City that leads to the High Energy Lab.

Note: you'll have to do this part of the Sunless City early in the Cycle of the Sun Explosion, as the sands will need to be fairly low to access this point.

Head down to the staircase and make your way downward. Follow the path and fall down the staggered broken floor of the building it leads to until you see a blue glowing cord leading out of the building and under a door with a switch.

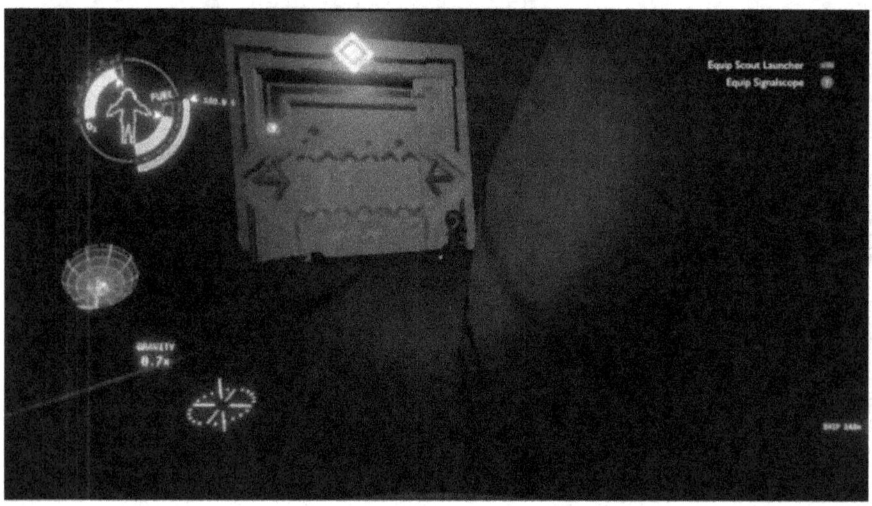

Open the door using the switch and continue to follow the blue cord until you come upon a sandfall with a wall of cacti resting above you behind it. Here, you'll have to wait for the sands of Ember Twin to rise above the cacti allowing you to continue forward.

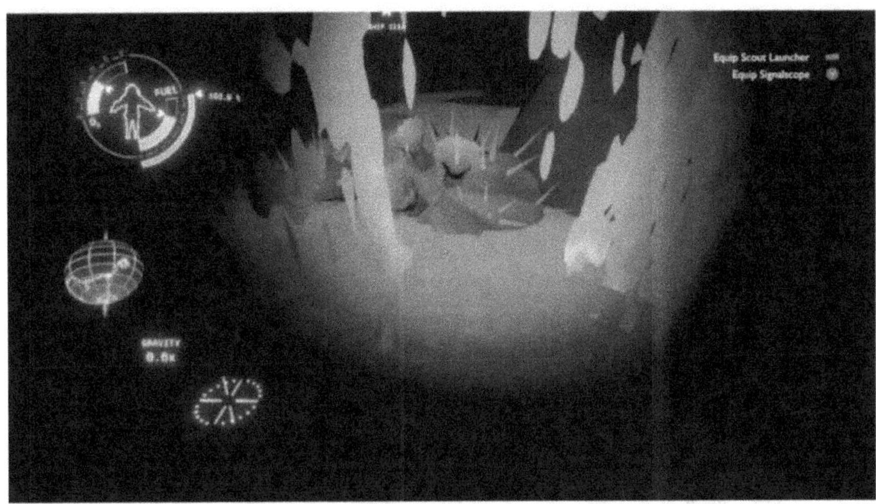

Once you move past this obstacle, continue following the blue cable until you come to an upward transporter. Hop in it and it'll take you up to a second level. The blue cord continues up into another transporter, only this one moving downward. Move past it and follow the broken path until you come to another upward transporter you'll have to boost into carefully.

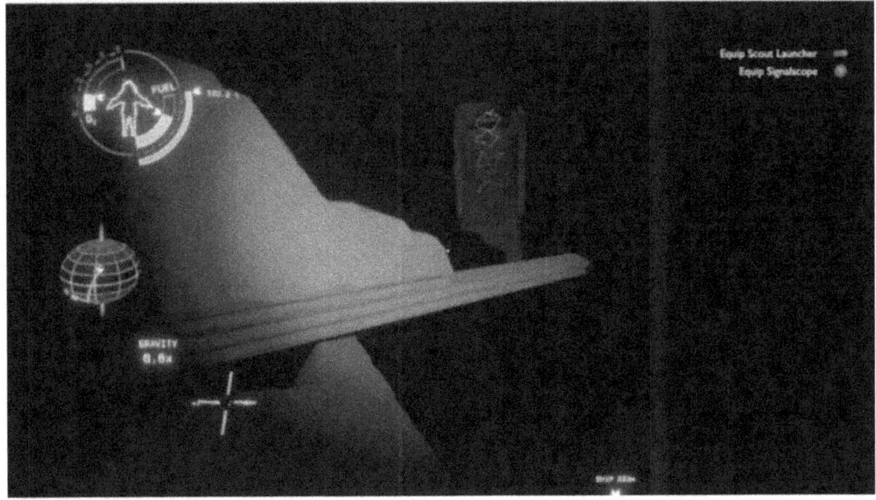

Once you do so you'll find yourself in the High Energy Lab.

Here if you read all the scrolls currently in the wall along with the one on the shelf, it details a tested theory about the findings of the White Hole Station, and concluded that they could cause objects to arrive in one location before leaving another, and with the right amount of power, could change the interval of that time. However, the power needed to cause this to happen lead to the creation of the Ash Twin Project, as well as an Advanced Warp Core.

Via the images on the wall, we can also see and confirm any hypothesis, that the different buildings located on the Ash Twin each have a corresponding planet within the Solar System.

TIMBER HEARTH

Timber Hearth is the home planet of your character, and where you start the game. It features the introductory area where you get your bearings on the basics and controls of the game but also features many secrets of its own. After you get done with the basic beginning area, make sure to explore the rest of the planet to find these locations:

Dark Bramble Seed

Near the North Pole of Timber Hearth, you'll find a large crater with a strange spiked seed in it. A Hearthian nearby named Tektite is investigating it and passively mentions that he'll have to grab another Hearthian named Tuff who owns a scout launcher to explore inside the seed further.

Inside the seed with a scout launcher you say? You have one of those! Equip it with RB and then launch it into the interior white center of the seed. You can then see inside the seed with snapshots using RB.

Inside there's what appears to be a much more massive area than is plausible along with something that looks akin to an angler fish.

Quantum Grove

At the South Pole you'll find a clearing with a large black rock in it that moves whenever you aren't watching and emits a signal on the Quantum Fluctuations frequency.

There's also some panels nailed up with the poem, " It's always dark, The quiet shade, Across old bark, In the ancient glade,"

Nomai Mines

On the equator line of Timber Hearth you'll find a ruin with a yellow symbol on the ground very reminiscent of the one at the North Pole of Brittle Hollow.

Just east of this will be a path that heads down into a valley with a broken bridge you can cross if you have your suit equipped using your jetpack. The bridge heads through a waterfall you can pass through, and after doing so you'll find a cave that leads deep underground and to a door. Use the glowing ball and your curser to move it up and to the left to unlock the door and head deeper underground.

After heading inside, you'll come to a large cave with a lake down below and a blue transportation beam coming out of it. Make a right when the road dead ends and doing so, you'll come upon a gap in the path with a large waterfall.

You can choose to jump in the waterfall and take the blue elevating energy up out of the water, or you can jetpack around the waterfall and continue up the path.

Either way, you'll come upon an overhanging platform with several elements you can interact with. Firstly is some Nomai writing you can decipher.

Here you learn that the Nomai were using some of the minerals of Timber Hearth to create a protective shell around the core of Ash Twin, and materials were being taken from Ash Twin to create towers on the planet as well, all for something called the Ash Twin Project. It was also stated that the materials taken wouldn't affect any future life for Timber Hearth.

Further down the path, you'll find an Ash Twin Projection Stone.

This is one of several Ash Twin Projection Stones in the galaxy, including the one found in the White Hole Warp Tower.

Picking up the Ash Twin Projection Stone, you can place it into two places nearby. Firstly, on your left is a strange phenomenon. You can plug the Ash Twin Projection stone onto one of two small columns to your left. Doing so will allow you to see a strange vision of Nomai statues glowing at you, but should you move toward them, the vision fades away. Weird.

The second use for the stone is up ahead, where you'll find another pair of columns. Plugging the stone in here allows you to see some more Nomai writing on the wall in front of it.

Here you learn of the completion of the mining used for the protective shell and moving on into a stage of checking for holes in it, with the mining team moving over to Ash Twin.

THE ATTLEROCK

The Attlerock is a small ateroid orbiting Timber Hearth. Below you'll find the activities and puzzles associated with it.

South Pole: Eye Signal Locator

At the south pole of the Attlerock, you'll find a strange device, as well as an underground area hiding secrets.

Signal Locator

On the surface, you'll see a large platform with a small glowing ball you can navigate using the center of your view. The ball can be navigated into 4 separate compartments, each with an image of a nearby planet. When transferred to a compartment, circular rings shift around the platform outlining the corresponding planet.

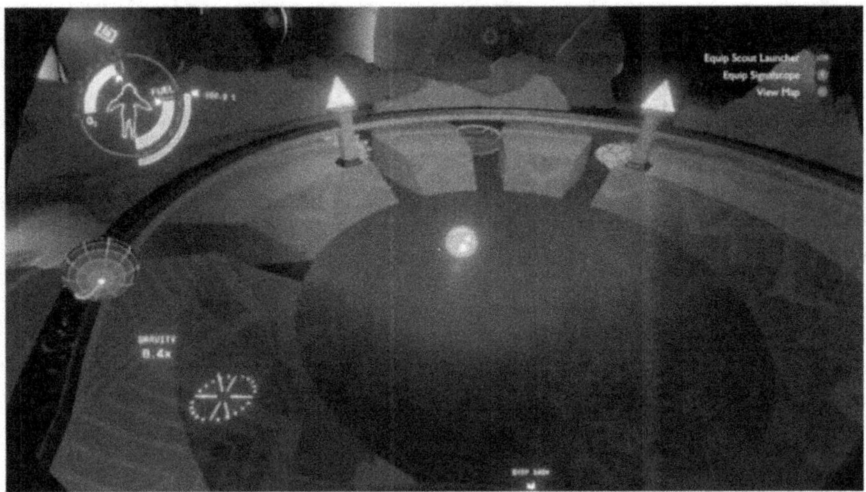

Yet one strange symbol has the rings circle, but not land on an object. Curious...

Nomai Decipher

You'll find a set of stairs nearby that can take you beneath the Signal Locator, where you'll find a room filled with trees that can refill your oxygen, along with a set of Nomai writings on the walls.

Upon approach of the text, you'll pull out your Nomai translator. Hold RB over the different swirls to decipher the text.

Upon translation you find that like you the Nomai couldn't get the Signal Locator to work on the "Eye's" signal, despite correct calibration. (We learn later that this refers to the Eye of the universe.) They decide that they need a more sophisticated device to access the Eye of the universe.

Strange Symbol

Across from the wall text, you'll find a strange triangular symbol on the opposite wall like the one the swirling text came out of on the other wall you just deciphered. However this is just a hole for a nearby scroll. There's some shelves on your left with a scroll you can insert into this hole to view what it says.

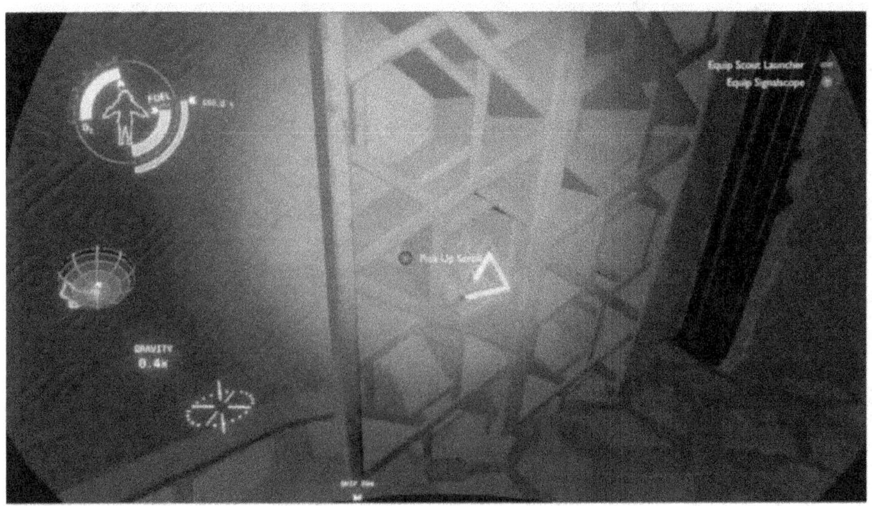

Upon insertion and decoding you learn that the Nomai discussed where to build a new more sophisticated Eye signal locator. They discuss Ember Twin, where they have already built a Quantum Moon Locator (wink wink nudge nudge), though due to heat making construction of that difficult they decide instead on the South Pole of Brittle Hollow.

Esker's Camp

To one side of the planet, about 2.5 clicks south of the North Pole, you'll find Esker, a Hearthian, whistling jovially. Upon speaking with him, you learn that he mans the Lunar Outpost of the Attlerock, but with ships becoming more sophisticated and not breaking down as much, his post has become quite lonely, so now he keeps an eye on things. And plants trees.

North Pole: Lunar Lookout

At the North Pole of the Attlerock, you'll find a series of platforms that lead to a fantastic view of the whole Solar System, you can chart where you'd like to go next, or use your Signalscope to try to find other travelers on the distant planets.

Reading Esker's notes at the site, you find that he heard something strange akin to the missing explorer Feldspar's harmonica through his signalscope coming from Timber Hearth. He brushes it off but maybe you should explore further?

BRITTLE HOLLOW

One step further from the sun than Timber Hearth, Brittle Hollow features an orbiting volcanic moon Hollow's Lantern that sends frequent meteors that slowly destroy it. Below you'll find the different points of note for this planet.

The Black Hole

At the center of the falling-apart Brittle Hollow is a massive black hole swallowing up the pieces of planet broken off from the meteors sent by Hollow's Moon. You likewise can be swallowed up should you fall from the many different platforming sections it takes to traverse this planet. Should you succomb to the black hole, it can take you to the far end of the system to the White Hole, so be careful.

If you wish to fall in and go to the White Hole, rest assured there is a way to get back so warp away.

How To Get To Riebeck's Camp

Finding the explorer on this planet Riebeck can be a hassle, since he's near the center of the planet underground. However, taking the time to do so can be rewarding because of the fact that he has access to many other places of note (even though he doesn't realize it).

To get to him you'll want to land at the Tower of Quantum Knowledge.

There is a way to go inside and reach the top of the Tower, but it's a bit complicated so we'll save that for later.

Head down the spiral staircase attached to the outside of the tower that leads you underground. Immediately ahead you should see a blue elevator that will bring you down to the base of the tower.

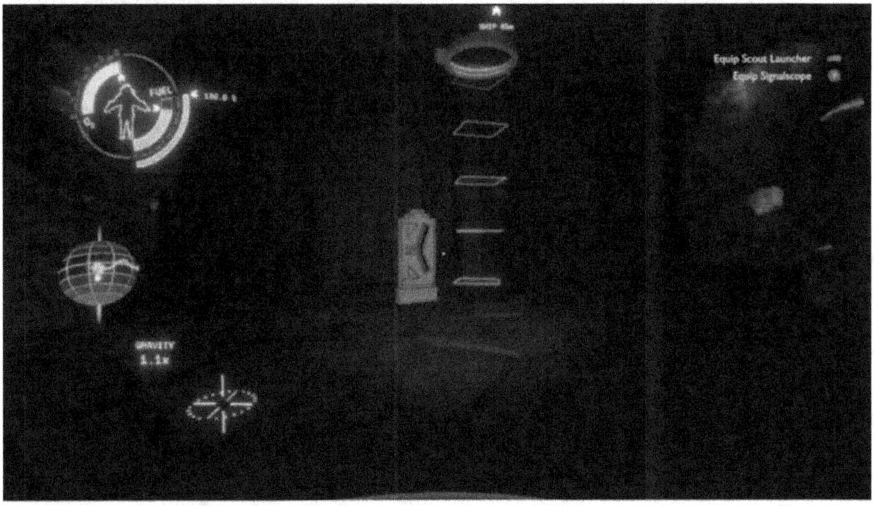

Head through the tower and make a right to find a another transport ring with a switch beside it. Use your cursor to move the switch into the up position and make your way through the series of transporters.

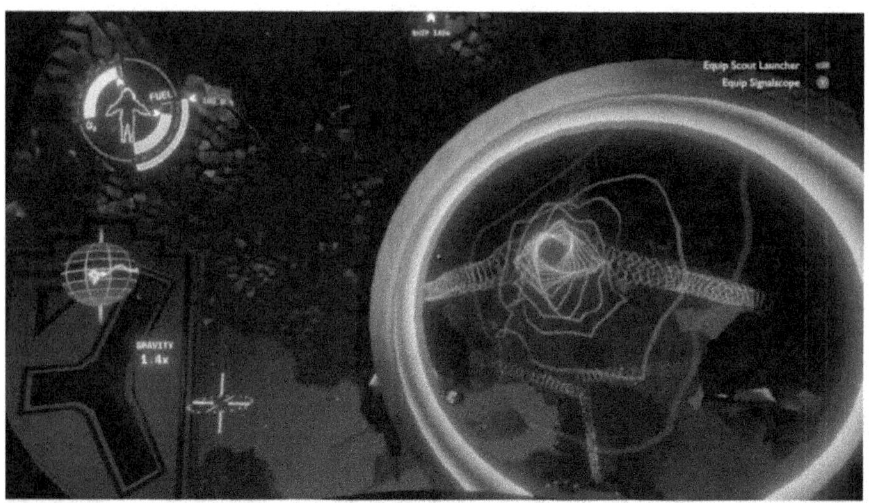

Eventually you'll come to a platform and hear a lovely banjo melody playing. You'll find Riebeck in his camp to your left.

The other route to Riebeck is a bit more random, but there's a transport beam aimed at the Black Hole at the center of Brittle Hollow. Should you find yourself falling toward the black hole, it is possible to direct yourself into this beam and reach Riebeck this way as well.

Northern Glacier

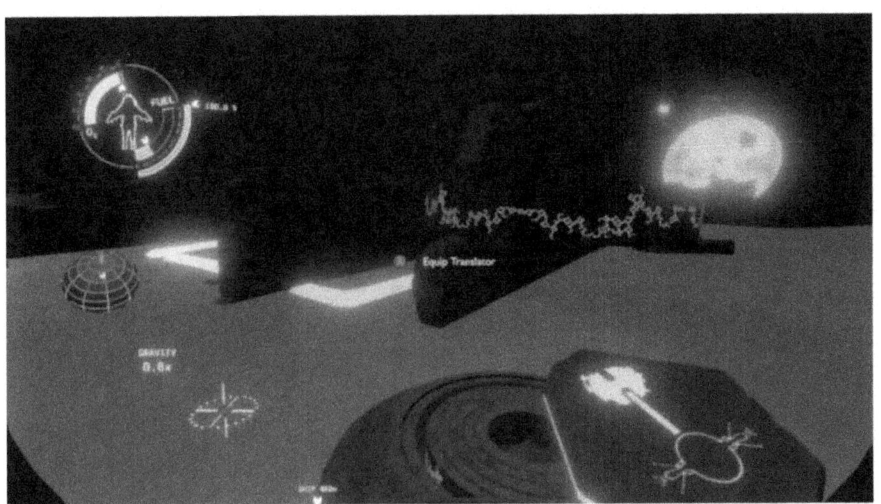

Located near the North Pole of Brittle Hollow, this glacier features a uniquely shaped Nomai Ruin. This is where you'll be teleported back from the White Hole Warp station.

Nomai Deciphers

There are several different texts to decipher in this area with your Nomai Translator. First up is a ring floating near the strange glowing yellow symbol on the ground.

It shows an arrival time a split second BEFORE the departure time. Strange.

In the ruins of a building nearby, there's also some Nomai deciphering to do. You'll find a strange hole in the ground with a ring embedded in it, and a wall in front of it that when translated reads, "The Hanging City (Below 50m)."

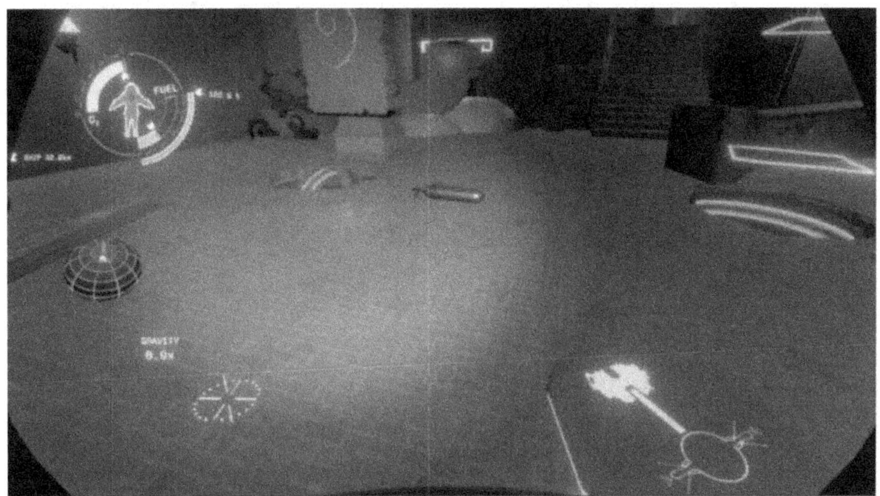

To your right is also an elevator beam that moves up. Must be something underground? We'll return to that later.

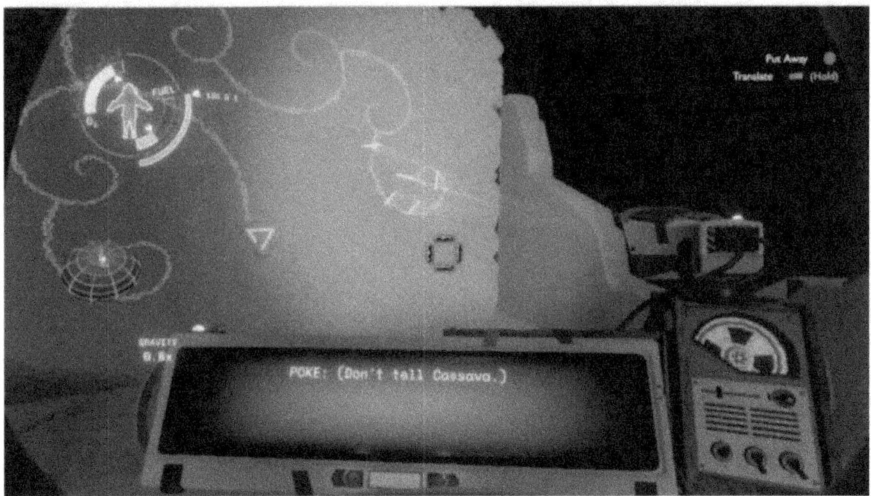

Up the stairs behind the elevator beam, you'll find a series of Nomai writings explaining the success of the warping from the White Hole station back to Brittle Hollow. However, they too noticed the discrepancy with the time of arrival being BEFORE the time of departure. You learn they returned to the White Hole station to double check diagnostics.

To your left head down the stairs. Here you'll see two strange looking small columns, one with an image of Brittle Hollow on it, the other with a hole that looks to be filled with some kind of object.

To use this you'll need to have a Projection Stone. There are several to be found throughout the solar system, however the easiest one to grab for our purposes is on a table in the White Hole Warp Station, so head through the black hole now if you haven't and return with the stone.

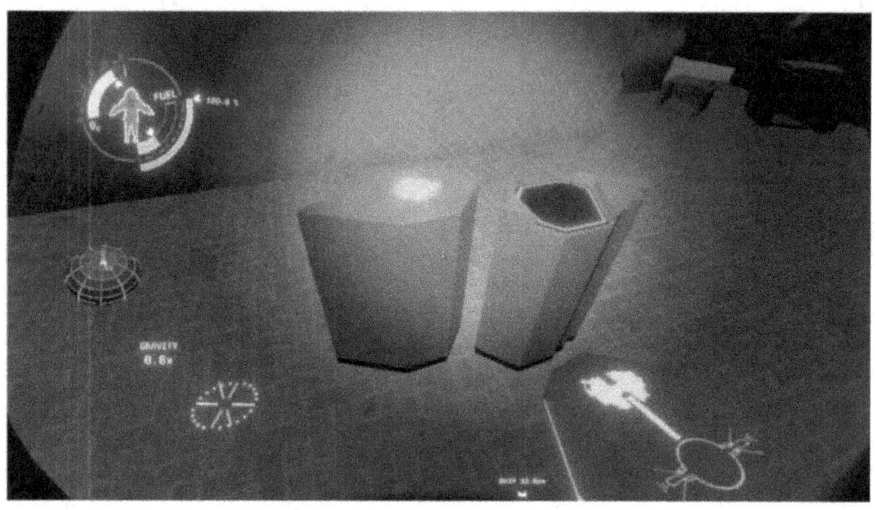

Inserting the Ember Twin Projection Stone into the hole, Nomai text appears on the wall in front of you. It reveals the confusion of the Nomai at the time differences of the warping, and they agree that they need to run more tests at a High Energy lab to gain more data. The final text is a call to action to get to the High Energy lab (located in the canyon on Ember Twin's equator) ASAP as something astounding has apparently happened.

Escape Pod 1

Near the equator line of Brittle Hollow, you may find your Signalscope picking up a strange signal. Following it, you'll come to a large alien spacecraft.

Outside, you'll find a long wire leading to a distress beacon and a small Nomai audio recording on the ground you can translate with your Nomai decoder.

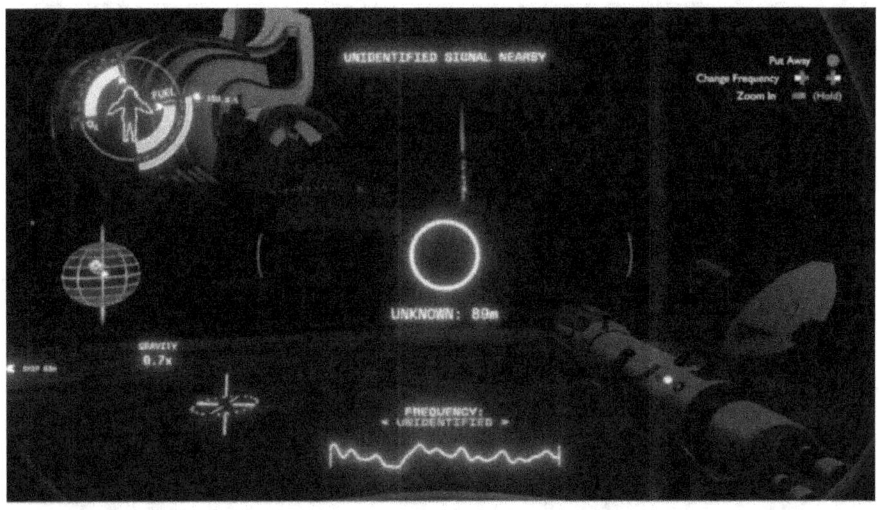

Decoding the audio, you learn of 3 Nomai escape pods existing, and that the Nomai that landed in the pod near you decided to try and find shelter at the southern end of the planet.

Inside there's a pole you can read that describes the crash of a Nomai Vessel, with three escape pods being deployed.

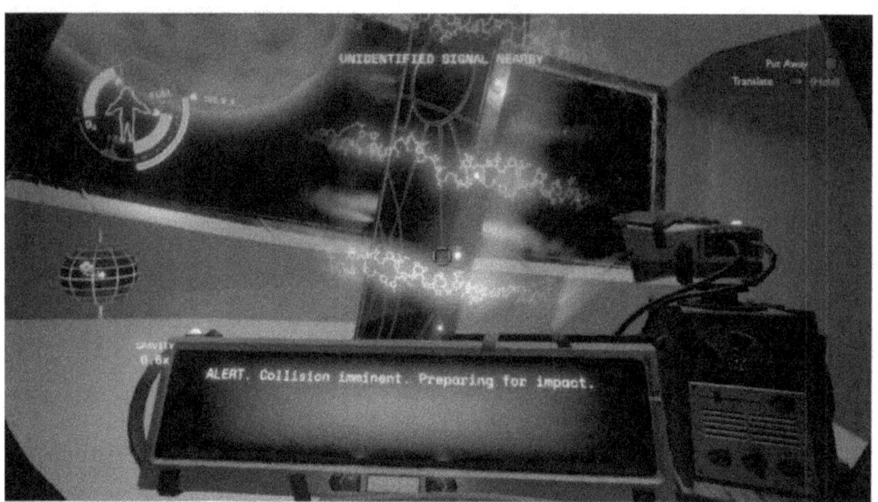

Old Settlement

Further inside the Escape Pod, you'll come to what appears to be a hatch with a ball in a swirl pattern you can unlock using your cursor. The text above it when deciphered reads, "Emergency Escape Hatch."

After moving the ball to the center center of the spiral the door will shoot off, revealing a large chasm with wooden platforms built into the side of the wall to aid you in moving downward.

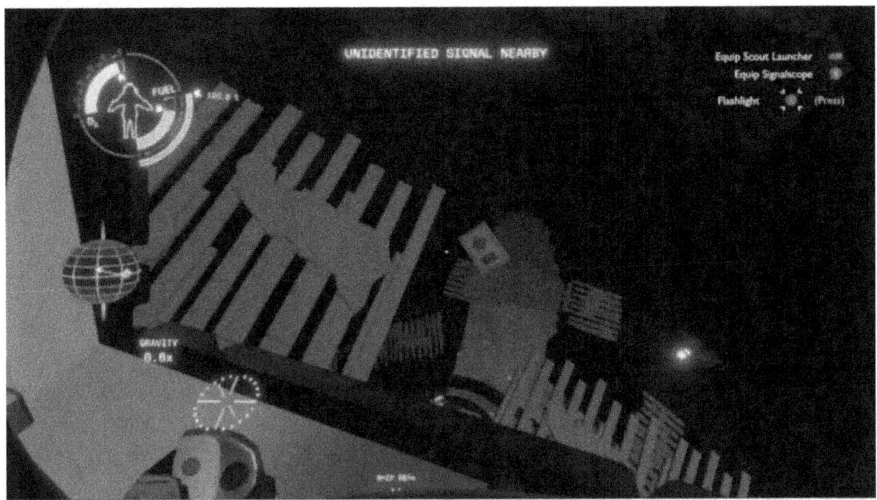

Carefully make your way down, avoiding falling into the black hole the lies beneath you. You'll see a short warning on the side of a wall that warns you as much.

Don't worry too much if you fall into the black hole. Just head on over to the White Hole page to learn how to get back onto Brittle Hollow.

Continue to make your way down until you arrive at an Old Nomai settlement they used as protection from Hollow's Lantern. You'll find a scrawl on the wall you can decipher, warning that while relatively safe here in the village to watch out for dust and decree falling from above. Heed this warning, as degree will begin to take out some of the paths to reach the different buildings in the Old Settlement.

Following the path, you'll come upon a wall with some Nomai writing you can decipher, with a wall with blue crystals to the left of it.

Deciphering the writing, the Nomai have decided that to continue their work, they'll need to make a more permanent living area here on Brittle Hollow, and decide to use gravity crystals to forge a safe path the southern glacier of the planet.

These gravity crystals mentioned in the writings are actually the blue glowing crystals on the wall. We'll return to this in a moment, but first let's take the time to explore the temporary settlement to see what we can find.

Decipher: Nomai Search for the Eye of the Universe

On one of the walls in a building ahead, you'll find a symbol of the Eye of the universe, along with some information you can decipher that tells you of how the Nomai heard a signal from the eye, but that this signal was older than the universe itself. The want to understand this signal was what led the Nomai here.

Mural of the Crash

Continuing down the wooden platforms between buildings, you'll come upon a mural of what the Nomai saw happened to their Vessel as they crash landed.

In the first image, you can see the Eye of the Universe calling out to the Nomai and their Vessel, in the second, you see something akin to the Dark Bramble taking ahold of the vessel. In the third, it's clear that the Dark Bramble still holds the vessel and one of the three escape pods, while the other two made their way to the Ember Twins and Brittle Hollow.

A nearby decipher explains that there shouldn't have been any problem with the Vessel itself, but rather, their destination which caused the initial issue.

Messages to Family Members

You'll also find a few messages to family members of those who crashed on the planet. One questions where his brother was in the mess of a situation and if he made it on board an Escape Pod. Either way he resolves himself to not let the loss of so many of his people be in vain.

Another note from the Nomai Thatch, asks whether it will be harder not knowing who they lost, or finding out later.

Gravity Crystal Path

Return back to the wall with the gravity crystals on it. This will act as your first path toward the Hanging City hidden within Brittle Hollow. There's multiple ways to access it, but we'll focus on this one first.

While next to the wall jump up and your feet will attach to the wall the crystals come from. Once attached to the wall, be careful not to jump outside of the range of the gravity crystals, or you'll likely fall into the black hole below.

Continue to follow the path of crystals until you come to be sandwiched between two walls of ice and yo come to a dead end of the crystals. However what appears to be a dead end is only a change of direction. If you look up, you'll see another line of crystals above your head.

Boost upward with your jetpack and you'll attach to this new wall and can make your way upward or should we say downward? Directions are hard with gravity crystals. Continue downward(?) until you come to some old ruins you can reground yourself too. Congratulations, you've found yourself in the Hanging City with a whole new area to explore.

Hanging City

If you've followed the guid thus far, then you arrived at the Hanging City via a gravity crystal path from the Old Settlement. However, this is not the only entrance into the Hanging City. Let's go over the others really quickly before we move on to exploration as they can expedite getting back to the city should you need to (which you will in a moment).

Hidden North Pole Entrance

In the Northern Glacier, you can find a hole into the ground found on one side of the broken structure in the streams of water. Location depected form an aerial view here:

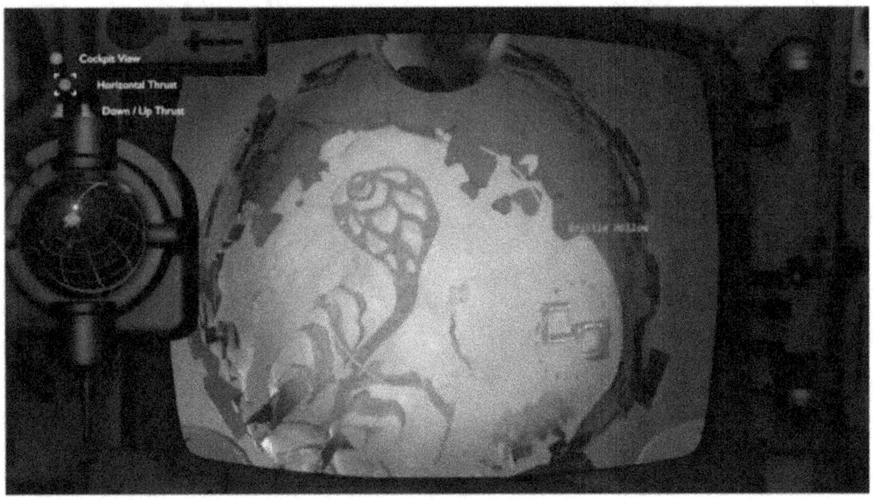

Navigating through the water streams, you'll find the water leading into a hole that drops down into an alcove with some stairs, and an transporter that will move you down into the Hanging City into the Meltwater District. More on that in a minute.

Bridge Entrance

From Riebeck's Camp, you can turn around to find a path of gravity Crystals on a wall east of the camp. Following the path of crystals laid out up the wall, you'll come to a platform that lies above Riebeck and his camp. Here you'll find a vague map of how to access other important structures located on the planet, and to your left will be a bridge that takes you to the Hanging City.

Note: Because Brittle Hollow is constantly falling apart, depending on how late into the cycle of the explosion you are, you may not have enough bridge to reach the Hanging City.

Exploration

The hanging city is divided into 4 distinct levels, which you can see by deciphering the large slab near the bridge should you come from that entrance.

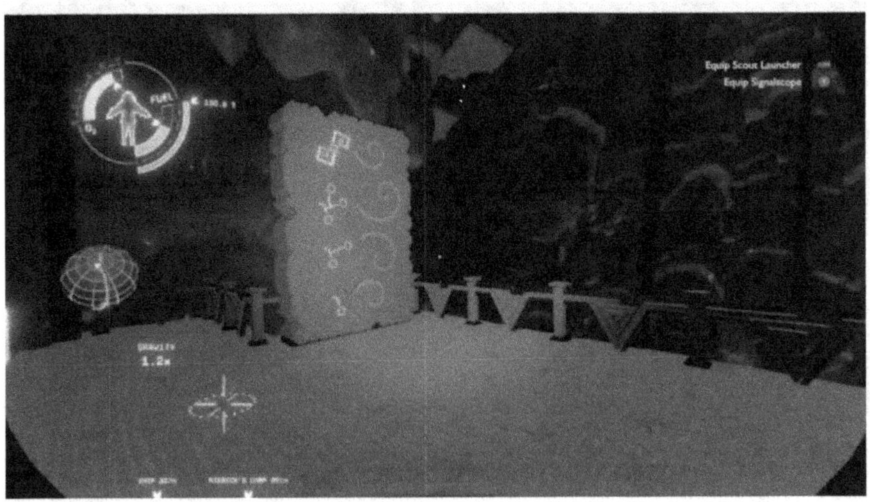

1st Floor - School District

2nd Floor - Meltwater District

3rd Floor - Eye Shrine District

4th Floor - Black Hole Forge District

Note that if you enter through the Bridge Entrance, you'll find yourself in the Meltwater District.

Throughout the district you'll find notes of a Black Hole Forge being built. This is our intended destination so keep this in mind for later.

To access the various other districts, you'll find an elevator of sorts near the slab indicating what levels there are and the symbols associated with it. It may be hard at first to figure out how to use it, however, you'll quickly discover that the walls use the same technology as the gravity crystals allowing you to traverse vertically to the other levels, except strangely enough you can't access the Black Hole Forge District.

On the first floor you'll find remnants of where young Nomai were schooled while on Brittle Holow, while the third floor has an area of study centered around the Eye of the Universe and trying to uncover its mysteries, which they never did, at least not here.

However we must access the Black Hole Forge for the most important Information, so let's focus on that next.

The Black Hole Forge

Accessing the Black Hole Forge can be extremely tricky and there's many ways to meet your death along the way, but follow these steps and you'll be unlocking its secrets in no time.

How to Access The Black Hole Forge

Starting from the Meltwater District of the Hanging City, you'll find two sets of stairs that lead you down into a room with a switch on a large cylindrical glass wall. Trigger this switch using your cursor to raise the Black Hole Forge back up to the top of the Hanging City.

However to actually get inside of the Forge, we're going to need to head to Ash Twin, so hop in your ship and fly there.

On the equator of Ash Twin, as the sand is removed from the surface of the planet, you'll find a building with a blocky silhouette and cactus atop it shown here:

Inside once the sand drops far enough, you'll find a gravity wall you can use to access a receded room beneath the initial room you entered. Inside this basement room, you'll find a floor of glass with a Black Hole Teleporter. Stare at the center of the floor as the planet rotates and eventually you'll be teleported into, you guessed it, the Black Hole Forge.

Inside The Black Hole Forge

Once inside the Black Hole Forge, make sure to carefully follow the path WITHOUT jumping, as your currently upside down, and will fall into the black hold of Brittle Hollow if you aren't careful.

Inside the building you learn a bit more about the Ash Twin Project, and the transfer of Cores for Black Hole Transportation. However the most important thing of note you learn is that there is something called a "High Energy Lab" on Ember Twin, perhaps this is something we should explore further.

Tower of Quantum Knowledge

Just south of the equator, you'll find the Tower of Quantum Knowledge. This Tower contains vital information on the third rule to access the 6th location, as well as the importance of the voyage to the Quantum Moon for the Nomai.

However, trying to access the tower while it's on Brittle Hollow will prove futile, as the gravity wall used to get to the top of the tower has been broken, making your path there broken as well.

If you've spent some time on Brittle Hollow, by this point you probably know that the planet is crumbling by the minute from the meteors sent from Hollow's lantern. These pieces fall into the black hole beneath and are taken to the far reaches of space! (So guess what we'll need to do)

Land on the top of the Tower of Quantum Knowledge. Nearby you can decipher a hypothesis from the Nomai regarding the Quantum Shards and guessing that these shards come from the Quantum Moon.

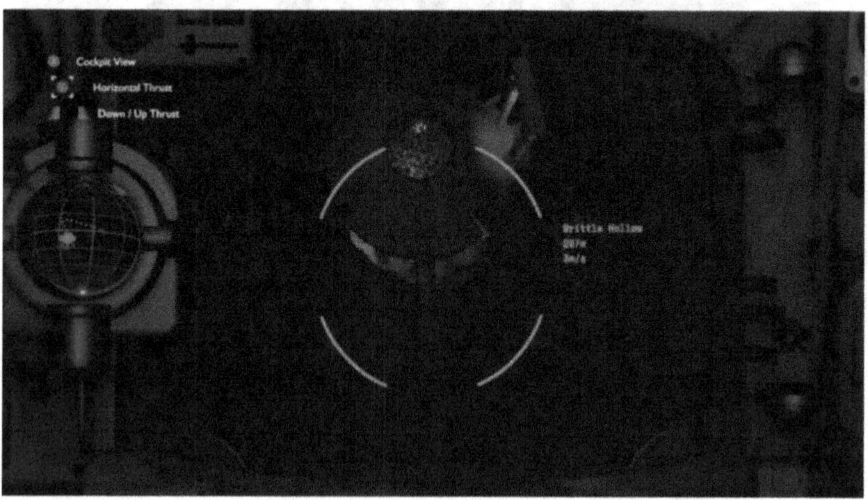

After this decipher, it's time to play the waiting game. Hop back in your ship and buckle in, and.....hang out. Eventually a meteor from Hollow's Lantern will come and break the earth beneath you causing the Tower of Quantum Knowledge to fall into the black hole beneath you along with your ship.

After you find yourself at the far reaches of space, find the shard of Brittle Hollow with the tower on it and land on it once again. Now that you're in zero gravity, there's no need to use the gravity wall to access the top of the tower.

Head inside through the base and up to the top. There will be two deciphers here giving you some very important information. The first will already be on the wall for you to translate, but the second you'll need to grab a scroll and insert into the wall before receiving your information.

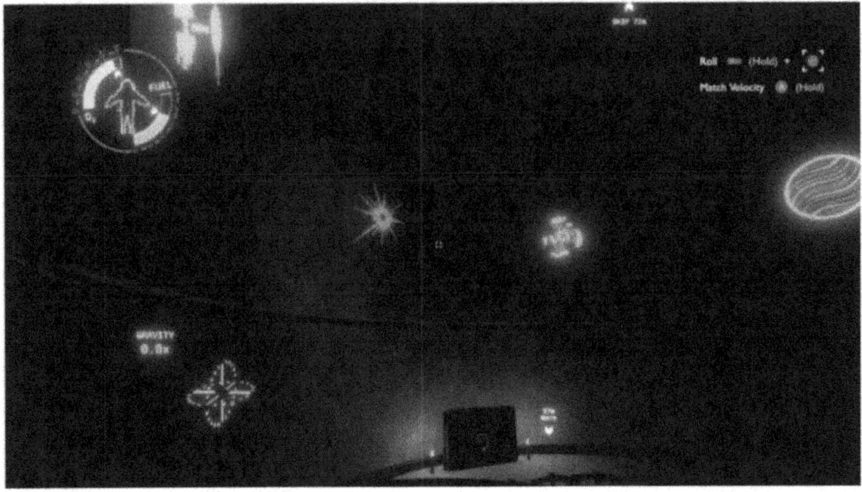

The two together explain how the voyage to the Quantum Moon was an important right of passage for the Nomai and that there's a shrine on the moon to help along the journey. It also tells you the third rule to accessing the 6th location:

The shrine must be on the moon's north pole.

The Southern Observatory

You may .have read from the various translations you've seen so far of the Southern Observatory located on Brittle Hollow. However trying to get there proves to be one of the more difficult location to access on the planet.

How to Get to the Southern Observatory

Approaching Brittle Hollow, you'll want to land on the Tower of Quantum Knowledge. This will be our starting point to arrive at the Southern Observatory using a secret path found underground.

Head down the stairs encircling the building. Once at the bottom, then continue right around the building. You should come to a gap with a set of stairs on the other side of the gap.

Jump it using your jets and head down the stairs. You'll come to two transporter beams along with a switch that controls them. Throw the switch into the Up position and head through the beam on the right.

This will launch you into the air, and you'll need to maneuver into one of the two beams ahead of you mid air. Don't miss your mark!

Once you are caught in one of the two beams, you'll be transported safely to a new platform. Walk around the column the platform is attached to and use the gravity crystals to walk up the column landing on another platform. Continue heading South, jumping the gaps from platform to platform.

Eventually you'll come to an area covered in ice.

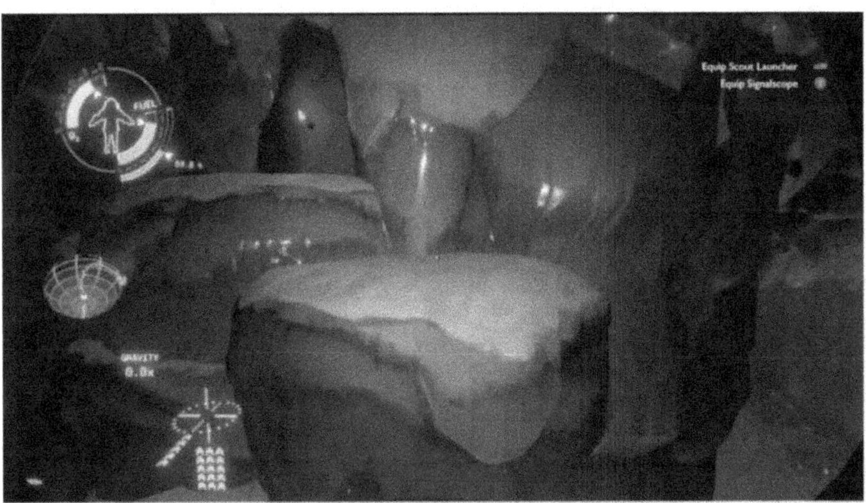

Across a gap you'll see gravity crystals in a line that you can use to climb up the face of the ice. Jump across and your feet will plant against the wall. Follow the path the crystals lay out and you'll come to a cloud of ghost matter you'll need to find your way around.

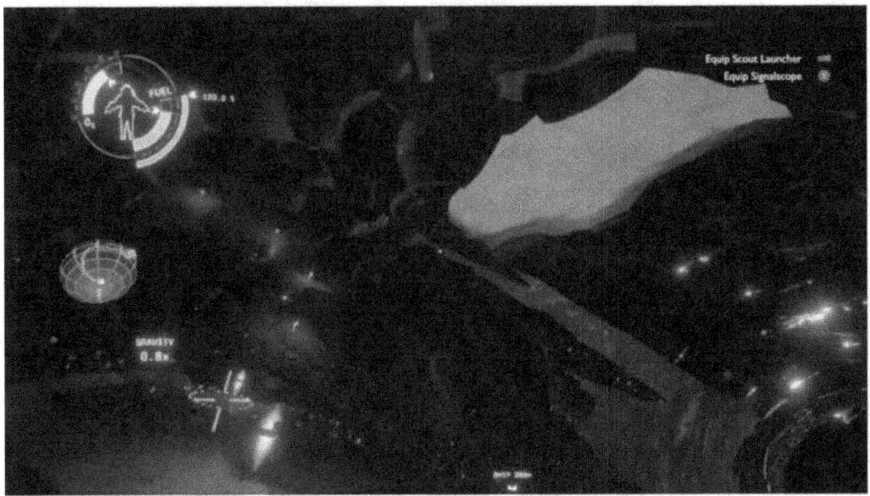

Thankfully on the other side of the chasm you should see an outcrop of land that you can boost to and then boost back over to the crystals, safely avoiding the Ghost Matter. After following the crystals a few steps further you'll arrive at a large opening with trees that will refill your oxygen.

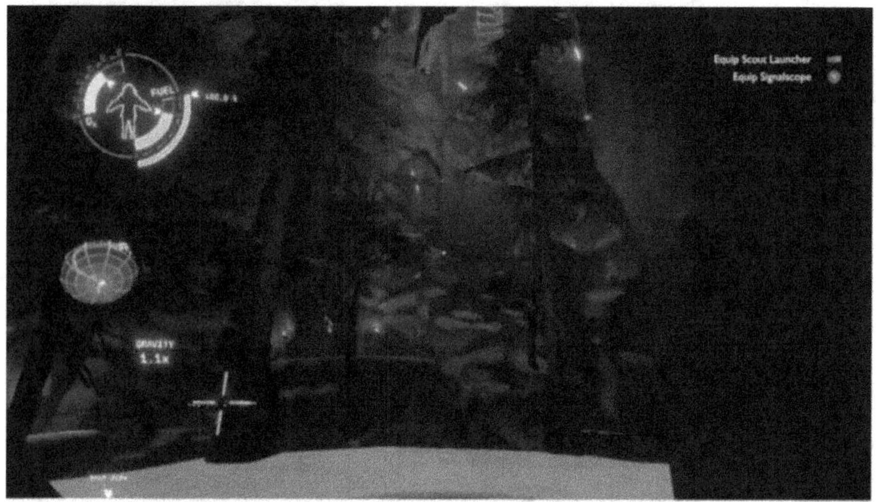

Head clockwise around the room, following the lamps on the wall, then jump the large gap to the opposite side where you should see another lamp, then jump back to where you should see a Nomai Ruin. Head into the ruin, and you can climb upward using the hole in the floor.

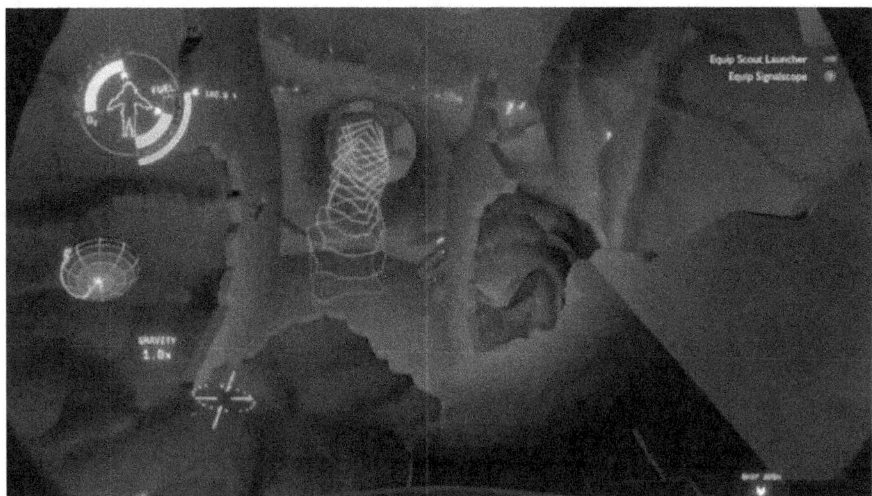

Lastly you should see a transporter beam in the roof that will carry you through the ceiling of ice and into the Southern Observatory.

Discoveries of the Southern Observatory

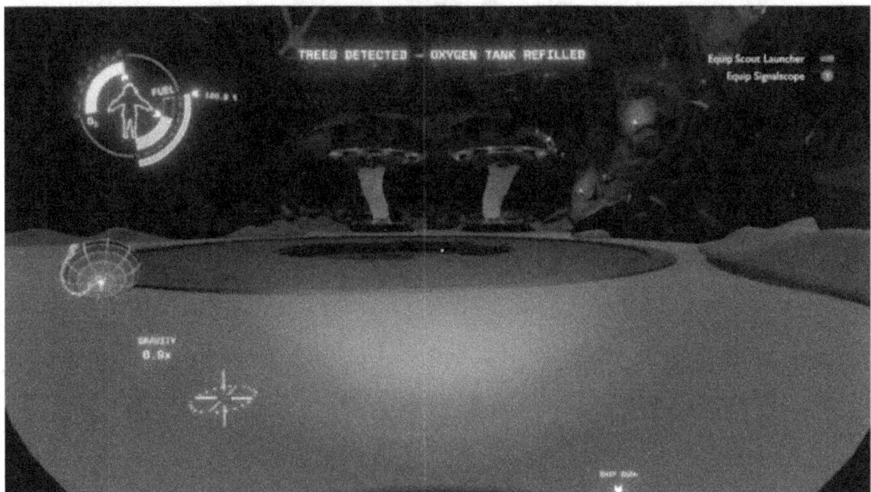

In the Southern Observatory if you dutifully uncover all the secrets there, you should learn a very important piece of information. Namely, that there are two types of cyclones found on Giant's Deep. If you've visited Giant's Deep you know there are several cyclones that move across the surface of the planet, shooting elements of the planet into orbit briefly. There's also a current beneath the surface that prevents you from swimming downward.

However, as discovered here at the Observatory, only the clockwise cyclones shoot things upward. If you enter into a counter clockwise cyclone, it will shoot you beneath the surface and past the current that keeps you from moving downward!

Upstairs you can also see some more writings based on trying to find the location of the Eye of the Universe, and that both the locator found Attlerock, and the more sensitive one found here both proved futile in the Nomai's search for the Eye.

They instead decide to build a Probe they can launch into space to try to find the Eye visually using the orbit of Giant's Deep.

GIANT'S DEEP

Giant's Deep is a planet swirling with tornadoes that shoot elements of the surface into space before gravity crashes back down to the surface. This page contains all the locations and secrets of the planet.

The Memory Statues

You have probably been wondering how you're continuously waking up in the same moment every time you die by your own hand or an as of yet unexplained supernova. That question at least, is about to be answered.

While hovering over Giant's Deep you'll see an island with a black hole teleporter on it (the giant orange glowing swirly S shape). Land in the blue beam here with your ship.

As you get out and make your way to the door, you'll find it busted from the outside. However, to your left is a gravity crystal path. Head there and use it to navigate yourself via a secret path into the building.

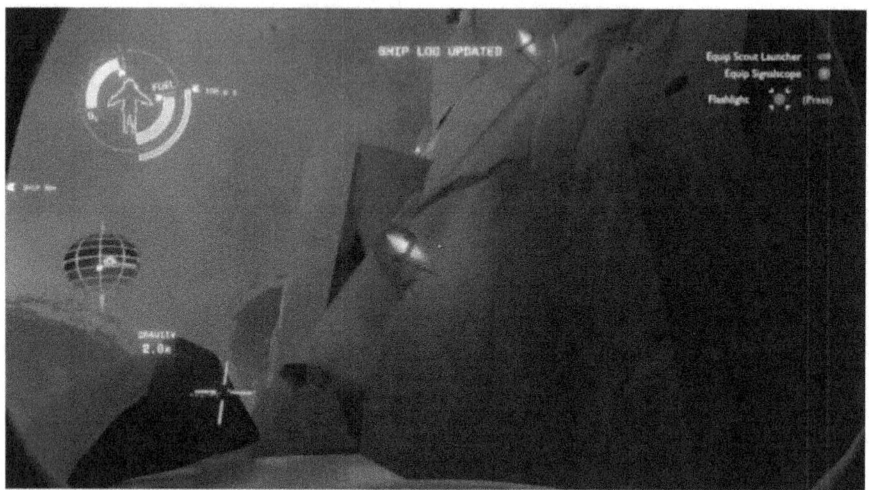

Heading through the buildings and out onto the large teleporter, you'll see a message greeting arriving Nomai, along with letting them know that the lab for this island lies beneath it.

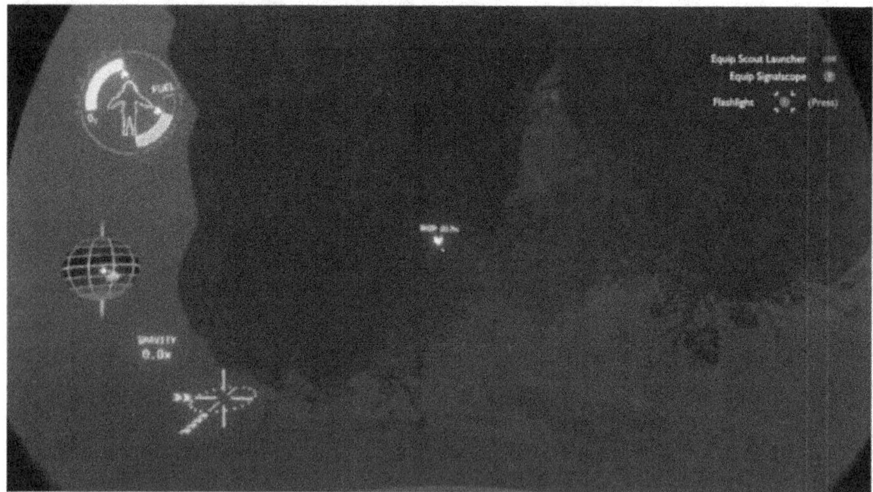

With this knowledge we can now head beneath the surface of the water and up into the recessed cave of the island.

There, using the Nomai Translator on a nearby recording, we learn the secret of the statue that looked at us at the beginning of the game. It's a device used to record the memories of Nomai, and using the Ash Twin Project, can relay those memories both past and future to whatever being the statue is paired with, which is why you're able to remember everything that happens before you die, despite being in the past. This allowed the Nomai to fix any issues on the Ash Twin Project before testing it.

The Tower of Quantum Trials

The Tower of Quantum Knowledge is a Nomai location that can be found on Giant's Deep that teaches players the first rule of Quantum Objects through a series of trials.

How to Access the Tower of Quantum Trials

The Tower can be found inside one of the swirling tornados found on the surface of Giant's Deep. Not just any tornado however, but the largest one on the planet's North Pole.

Head there and then simply use your thrusters to boost yourself up and over the wall of wind to come upon the Tower hidden inside.

Conquering the Trials

Once inside the tornado, land on the platform and head up the path to the left. Eventually you'll come to an transporter beam that will take you up and into the Tower.

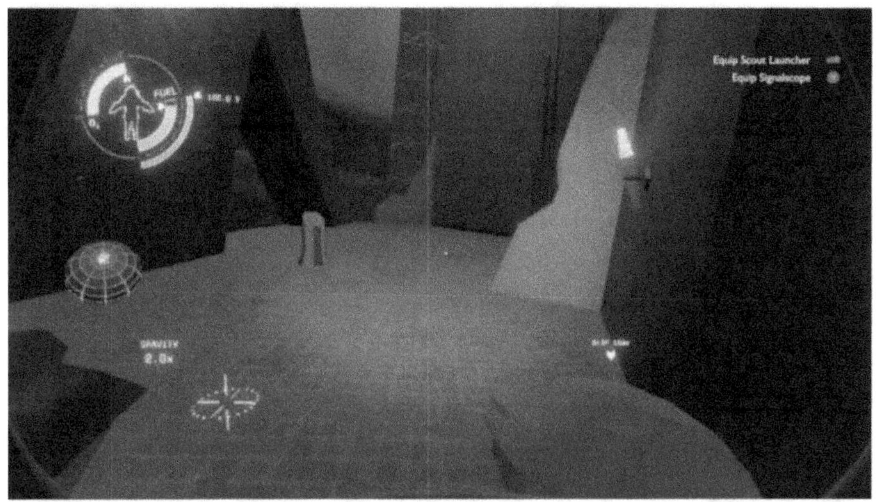

Inside, you'll find a large room with a Nomai message stating that these lessons are for you to learn for yourself. You'll also see an archway with a hole beneath it. Head into the hole to begin your first trial.

Inside a Nomai text will tell you to seek the wandering arch. You may notice a corresponding arch within the room that moves every time you look away from it. This is a quantum object, and you must keep your camera fixed on it as you move towards it. Doing so will allow you to access the hole underneath and progress to the next Trial.

Falling through the hole, you'll come upon a similar object that moves when you don't look at it. It is a shard of the Quantum Moon, but there is no Trial associated with this floor, so head through the hole in this room to progress.

The Nomai writing within the next room you fall into lets you know that observing an image of a quantum object and observing the object itself are one and the same. So in being able to photograph with your Scout, you may be able to guess where the solution to this problem lies. Once again you're faced with a wandering arch, however this time walls will always block your view of it. To keep it in the same place, snag a photo of the arch with your Scout and keep in front of your field of view as you move up the stairs to the arch's location. In having the photo of it, it won't move, and you can progress to the next riddle, falling through the hole under the arch.

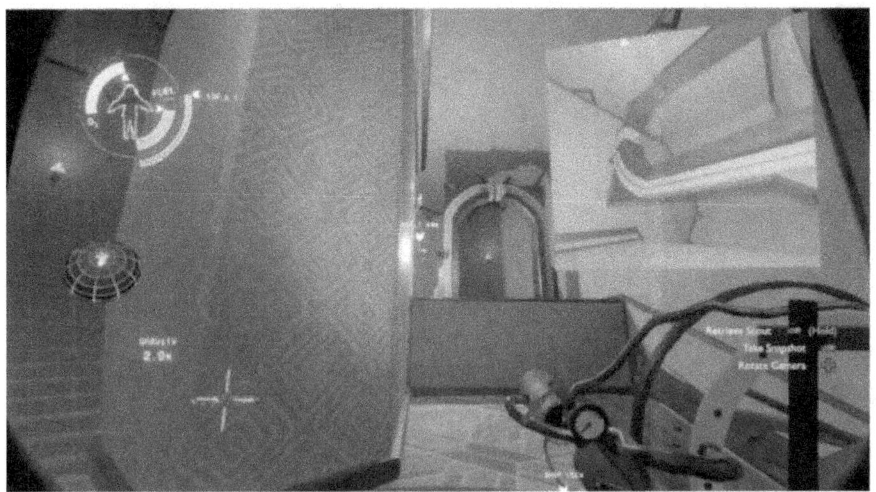

In the next room, a Nomai text informs you that the gravity crystal on one of the walls that allows you to climb one of the walls, and the arch that lies atop those walls do not meet naturally, and both objects are quantum and move around the room on their own.

To solve this puzzle, first take a photo of only the crystal on the wall, without looking at the top of the all. In doing so, the crystal will stay put and as you turn around, the arch will move around the room. Once the arch and crystal lie on the same location, photograph the whole platform, arch and crystal both, and then you'll be able to climb up and reach the arch, and head through to the next Trial.

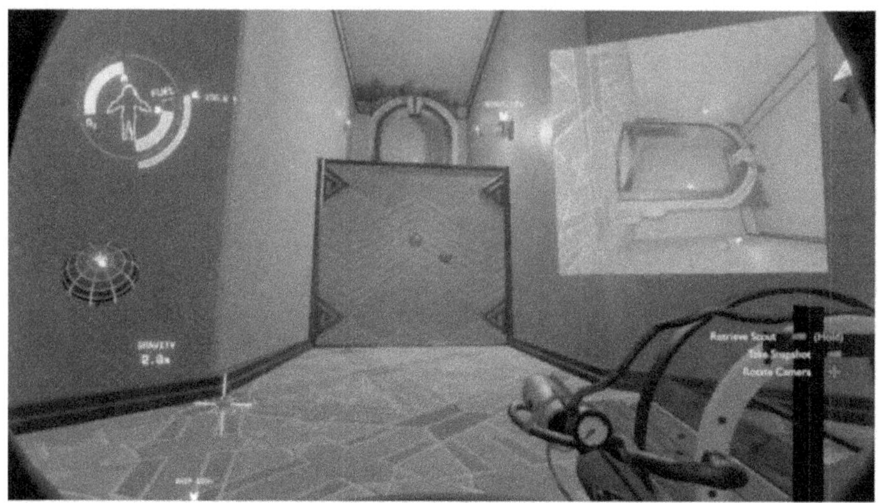

Note: you can also solve this puzzle by taking a photo of the arch once both are located on the same wall, and then fire your Scout above the wall to view the arch in the photo. Finally, avoid diverting your view from the crystal as you climb the wall.

As you enter this final room, the Nomai writing informs you as much but also mentions that it's a harder challenge. On opposite walls of the room, each has two quantum gravity crystals whose positions change each time you look away. Using your Scout, fire at one of the walls with the crystals in the bottom and middle row of the wall, then climb up to the middle section.

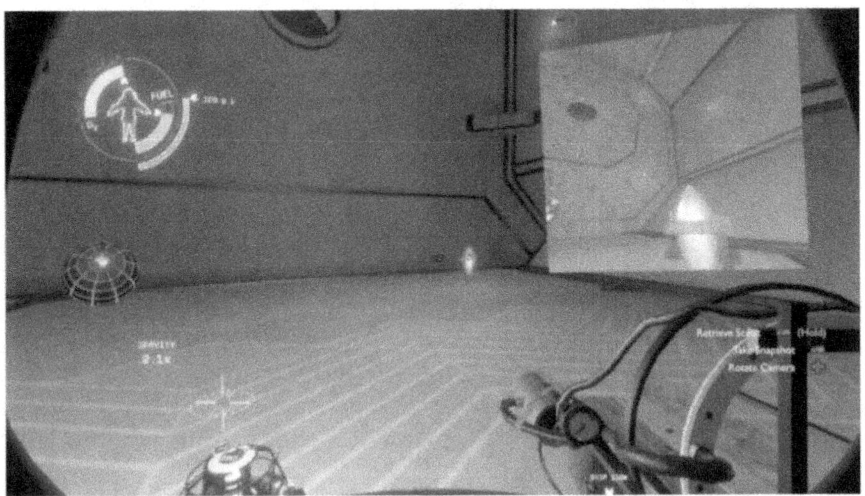

Once there, take a picture of the middle crystal but NOT the one at the base, then spin until the crystal appears in the highest row above you. Look directly at it as you climb up the wall and over the edge to reach the top platform.

You may find once you reach the top that the arch is on the other side of the room. However, this is no problem for a master of the first rule of quantum objects.

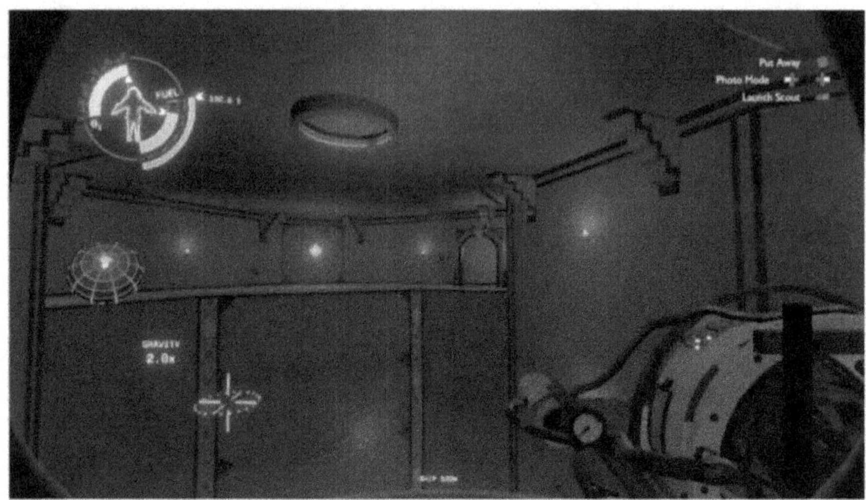

Simply spin around until the arch appears on your side of the room, then drop through the hole beneath it.

n the final room of the tower, Nomai writing on the wall congratulates you on your achievement, and simultaneously let's you know that the other shards also have lessons to teach.

So to recap the first rule of quantum objects:

Objects don't move as long as you are looking at them, and looking at a picture of the object and the object itself are the same thing.

Giant's Deep's Core

If you've taken the time to try and penetrate the deep water of Giant's Deep and come out the other side, you have probably found your attempts futile. However, there is a way to do so with a great secret hidden within.

How to Access Giant's Deep's Core

All across the surface of Giant's Deep you've seen the tornados that spin sending pieces of the planet shooting into space.

However, if you've explored the Observatory on Brittle Hollow, you may have seen that the Nomai discovered this upward movement only applies to tornadoes spinning clockwise. The more rare counterclockwise tornado will shoot objects down as easily as its counterpart shoots things up.

You may see where this is going now. Head into a counterclockwise tornado while in your ship, and you'll be sent deep below the surface of Giant's Deep's ocean.

However, here we're met with yet another conundrum. Looking down, you'll see a large electric core with red jellyfish floating above it. Trying to penetrate the core with only your ship again is a futile venture.

The knowledge of how to get in however, can be found on Dark Bramble. If you've encountered the Jellyfish Corpse there, you'll find that Feldspar went inside one of the jellyfish to travel into Giant's Deep's core. You may do the same! Approach a jellyfish from the base inside your ship, then rise upwards into the head, allowing your vision to be filled with the translucent red glow.

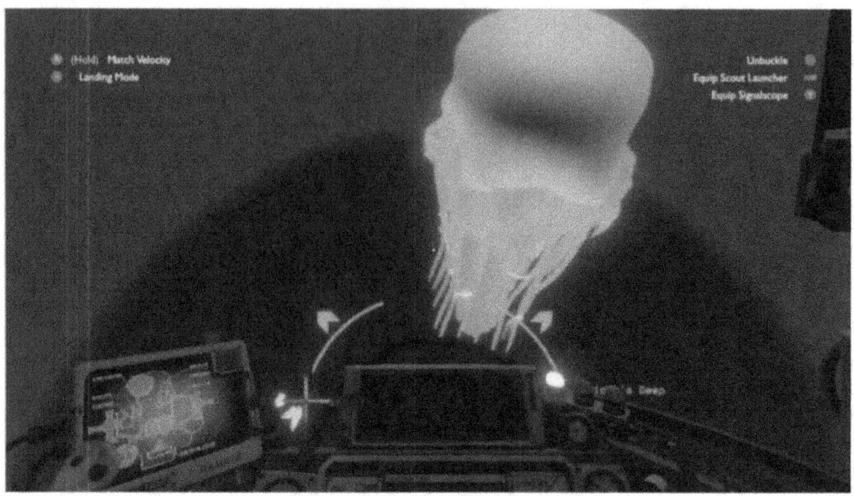

Once inside, the jellyfish will ferry you through the electric barrier, giving you access to the core of Giant's Deep and the secret area it holds.

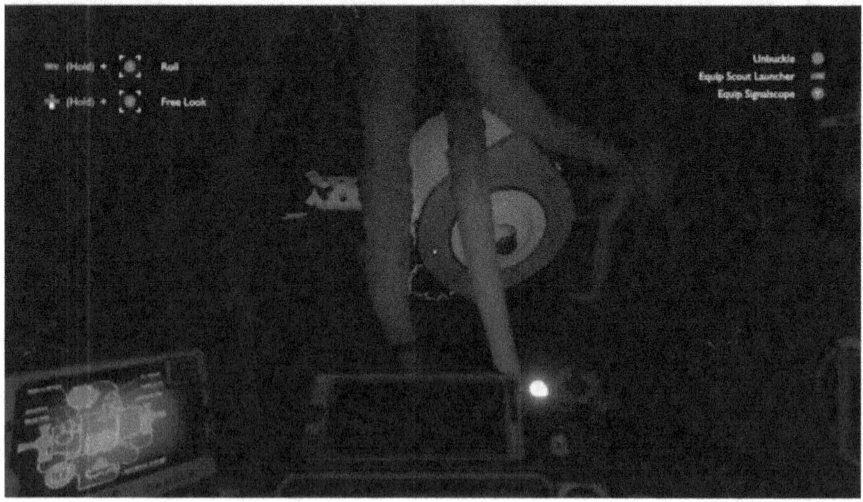

Inside, you'll see a large purple core with sprouting vines coming out of it. Attached to these roots you should see a Nomai structure. You'll want to land on it somewhere and make your way inside. To get in you should see a tube on the side of the building similar to the one used to enter the White Hole Station. Inside you'll find a switch to open a door to let you into the Probe Tracking Module.

Probe Tracking Module

Once inside the probe tracking module you'll find a ceiling and floor both with gravity walls as floors that allow you to walk on the surface of each.

Let's head to the one with the large tube sculptural object first. Using your cursor, to drag the ball into the first two switches, you'll be given a visually spectacular representation of the launch of the Probe Tracking Module. You'll learn that between combining the Memory Statues and these probes, they fired 9401 Probes with the 9354th finding criteria matching the Eye. The 4th and final switch will create a projection of 3 symbols.

These are the exact coordinates of the Eye of the Universe, and you'll need them later to reach the Eye.

On the ceiling you can read two separate Nomai conversations about the Probe with expectations and hopes high about the chances of receiving the Eye of the Universe coordinates.

DARK BRAMBLE

Dark Bramble is a dangerous, hazardous, and confusing planet, but a necessary voyage to discover some more secrets of this galaxy.

How to Find Feldspar

We know that Feldspar is lost somewhere within Dark Bramble, and we can hear him playing his harmonica when we listen through the Signalscope and focus on Dark Bramble.

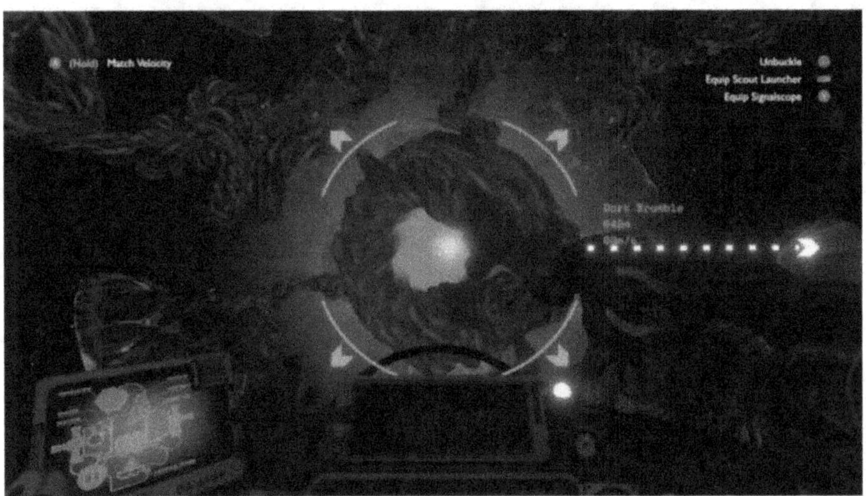

To reach him, fly into one of the white holes of dark bramble. There you'll see several bright white lights show up. One of them will continue to have the signal coming from the Signalscope. However be wary, as you'll find a giant hostile anglerfish in this area that will make its way to you and gobble you up should it hear the slightest noise.

However, we know from the fossil of an anglerfish found in the Sunless City on Ember Twin that anglerfish are blind, and as such will only respond to noise. Poised with this knowledge, reduce use of the jets on your ship to a BARE MINIMUM and make your way slowly but surely to the source of the Signalscope.

Eventually, you'll come to a seed with more glowing entrances in it. Dark Bramble is strange, and has rooms upon rooms of bright lights for you to traverse. Before you head into the seed, fire your Scout inside this seed, then proceed in.

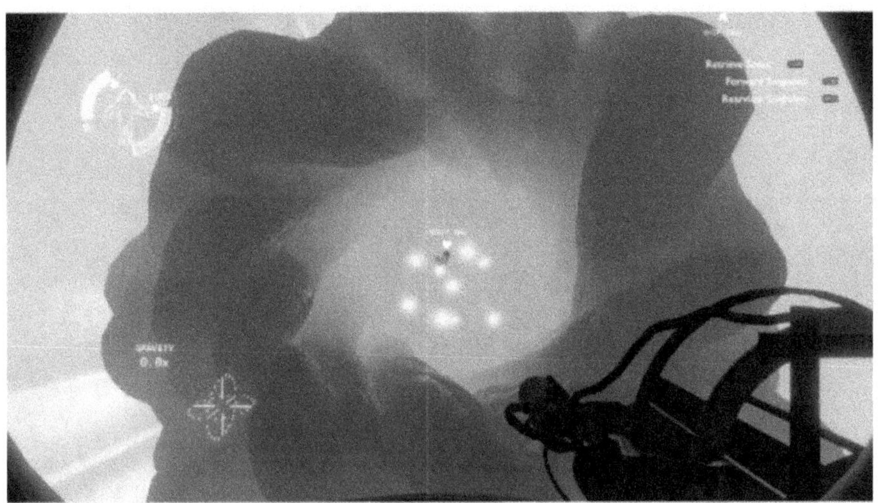

Once inside, you'll see that the Scout has scattered into three distinct signals. Follow the one on the far left, again making as little sound as possible.

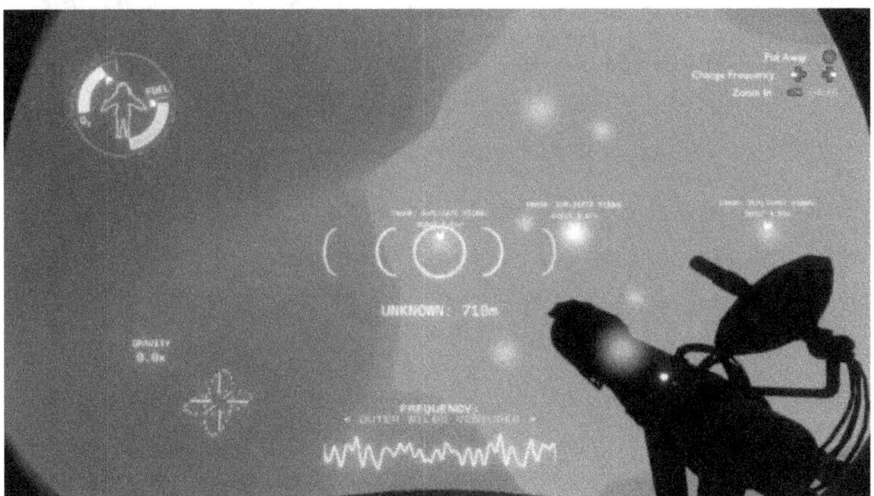

Once you reach the seed there, head on in, no Scout Required this time. On the other side, you'll be met with an anglerfish fossil you may remember from the Bramble Seed found on Timber Hearth. Inside this fossil you'll find the great explorer Feldspar!

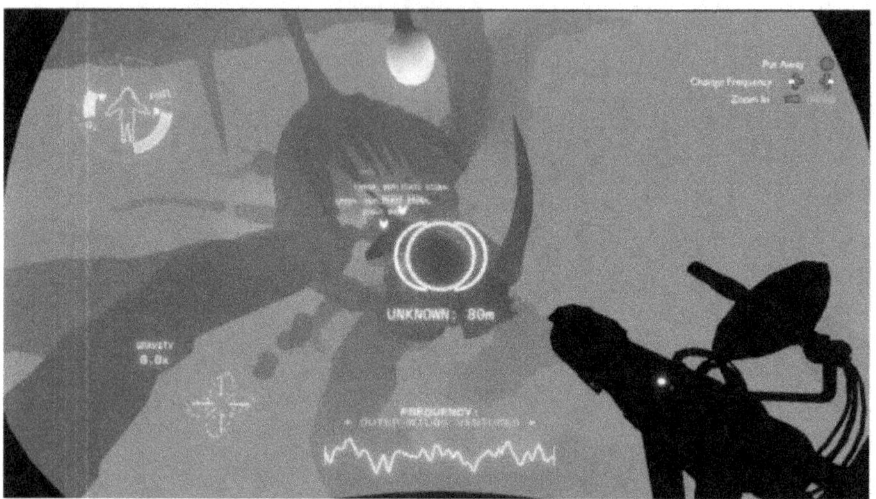

You can speak to him about his predicament and how you got here, but his best piece of information he holds secret from you, to find it, you'll have to follow the hint he gives.

How to Find the Jellyfish Corpse

Head back through the corpse of the dead anglerfish and toward the blinking light in the fog. You'll come upon Feldspar's crashed ship and the hollow vine it crashed through.

Head into the vine and make a left. Follow the hollow path way until you come to a dead end with a strange corpse of a jellyfish. These may be familiar to you if you've ventured into Giant's Deep.

Heading inside the jellyfish, you'll learn that inside the body of one of the monstrosities, you're immune to the electric current that runs around Giant's Deep's Core. Remember this information for when you return to Giant's Deep!

As we know from our explorations, the first and second escape pods from the Nomai Vessel landed on Ember Twin and Brittle Hollow respectively where the crews were able to escape and set up large communities and structures. However, the third was taken by Dark Bramble, and is now lost somewhere within its quantum seeds.

To find the 3rd Escape Pod you'll need to tune your signalscope to the Distress Beacon channel. If you haven't already used this channel yet, you'll need to go to Escape Pods on Brittle Hollow or Ember Twin and have your signalscope discover the signal, then you'll be able to use it again to find the distress beacon coming from Dark Bramble and follow it.

Once following the signal, head to Dark Bramble and head inside. Continue to follow the Distress Beacon Signal toward one of the bright white spots. Be CAREFUL! as there is an anglerfish in this area to worry about. Once inside use minimal thrust (1 tic) only when necessary to redirect yourself. Any more than that and the anglerfish will hear you. Once at the seed, continue through to the next area.

Once in this second seed continue following the distress beacon on your signalscope. You'll see far more roots in this area as you begin to approach what you'll discover to be the 3rd Escape pod.

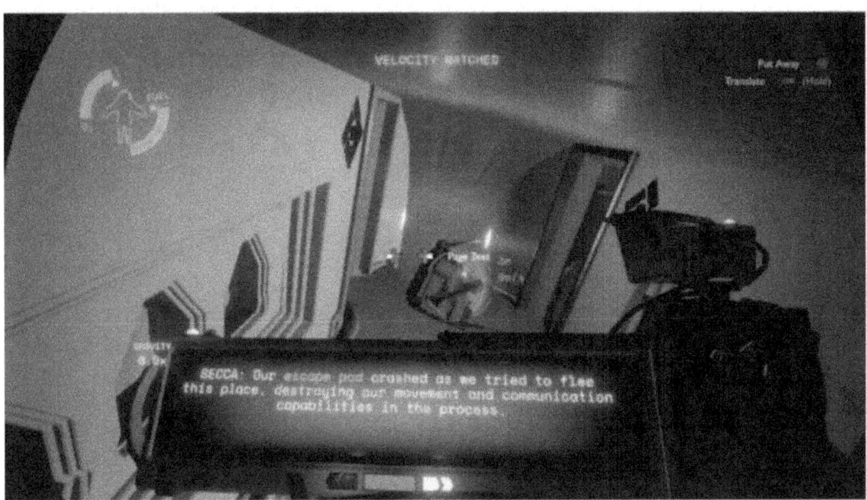

Head out of your ship and inside the Escape Pod where you can translate some notes about the Pod's crash landing and the Nomai quickly leaving the pod to find their Vessel, lost somewhere in Dark Bramble. A second note also makes it clear that the Nomai equipment is detecting two signals from the Vessel.

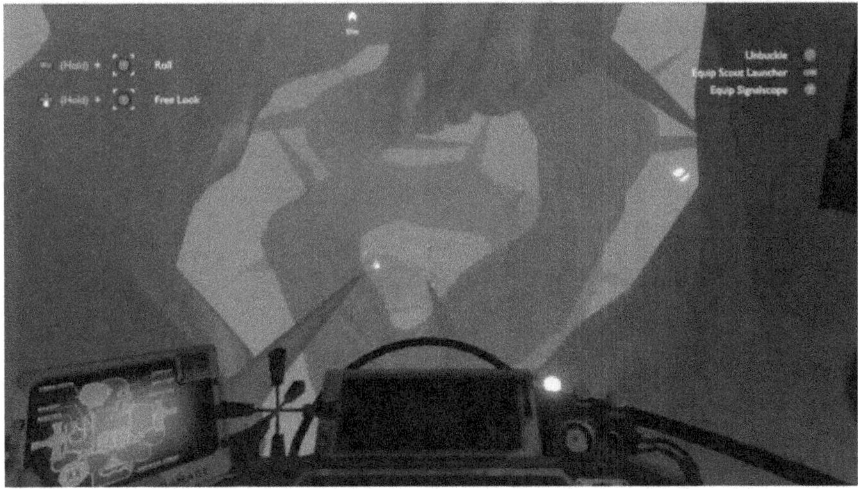

They don't have enough resources to reach the second beacon, making a decision instead to make it to the first, leaving a trail of lights from the escape pod to be able to find their way back or for other Nomai to follow them.

Finding the Vessel

Open the escape hatch out the back and hop back in your ship. You should see a trail of light cubes leading away from the Escape Pod.

Following these, you'll arrive at a seed with an entry point not wide enough for you or your ship to fit through, surrounded by the corpses of dead Nomai. A Nomai recording nearby states that the Vessel's signal is still faintly coming from inside the seed. They were lost as to the solution to this conundrum, but you have something they don't with your scout. Send it into the seed's opening and a new duplicate waypoint will be revealed beyond the horizon toward the glowing orange light behind the seed.

Hop back in your ship and carefully boost toward the orange light, where you'll find another seed you can enter. Boost into it, but after doing so, DON'T MOVE. On the other side of this warp, you'll find 3 anglerfish in a row waiting to gobble you up.

If you stand completely still, you can wait until they've vanished into the fog behind you as you move past. Once they've done so you can use your booster and one bar to boost forward towards your destination.

You'll find one last seed in this area to make your way through. Doing so you'll arrive at the famed missing Nomai Vessel!

Now that you know how to get here though, there's not too much we can do without a few other items, as you'll need a way to power the large ship.

WHITE HOLE

So you've been shot through the black hole on Brittle Hollow huh? No worries, there's actually stuff here to discover as well. Below you'll find the things of note for White Hole.

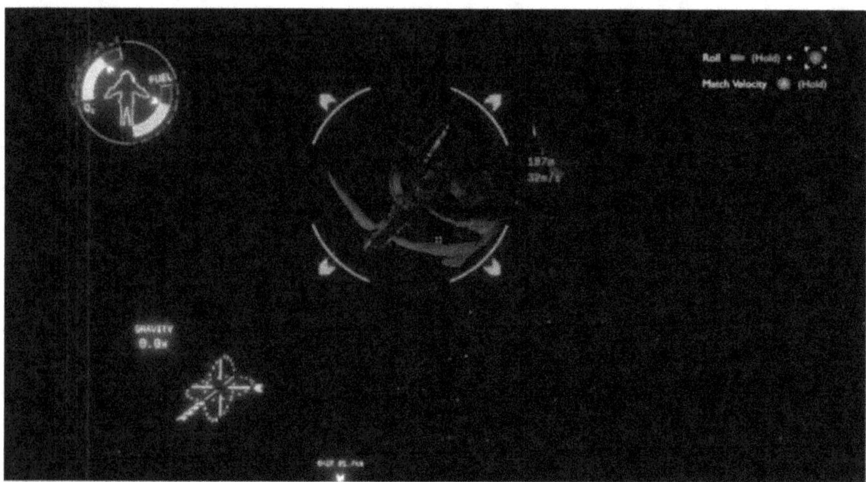

Hidden in the darkness of this area of space far away from the sun, you'll have to wander about a bit if the sun's light is being blocked by the many planets and objects between you and it.

In that darkness, you should see a large object that you can make your way to. This might be slightly challenging without having your ship and just using the flight controls of your suit so make sure to use the match velocity function to reach it unharmed before you run out of fuel.

In the center of the object is a cylindrical tower with an entry point in it. Making your way inside the tower, you'll come upon a small puzzle where you'll have to use your cursor to move a point of light around a pentagon. Do so and the door will open into the tower.

Inside you'll find a large room with two transporting beams on either side, a wall with some Nomai scrawling, and a symbol of the current station that you're on, with an arrow pointing to the left, with arrows above it pointing to a symbol of Brittle Hollow.

You'll also see an item called the Ember Twin projection stone on a nearby table that you can pick up and carry with you. Do so, you'll need it when you return to Brittle Hollow

Deciphering the text on the wall, you learn that this is a Warp Station used by the Nomai to teleport themselves back to Brittle Hollow should they fall into the black hole there like you did. It also says that to do so you'll need to stand in the center of the platform and look up when Brittle Hollow is positioned in the sky above. However, currently the station isn't rotating so let's work on that first.

One of the transporting beams will move you into a basement area below the platform, there you'll be able to use your curser to interact with a ball of light, moving it into one of two small areas the will trigger the rotational direction of the station.

After you've moved the ball into one of the diamond shaped triggers, head through the transporting elevator back up to the top. You'll notice now that the symbol of the station on the wall is also rotating.

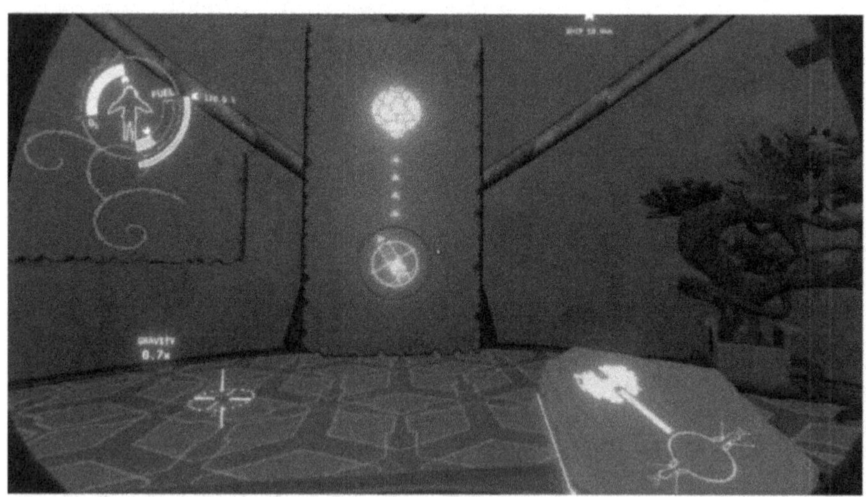

When the arrow lines up with the others pointing in the direction of the Brittle Hollow symbol, stand in the center of the platform and look up to teleport yourself back onto the planet with the large Black Hole.

QUANTUM MOON

The Quantum Moon is one of the Quantum objects found within Outer Wilds and a large mystery to unravel. If you wish to follow in the footsteps of the Nomai and their pilgrimage to the 6th Location, you'll need to head there.

Landing on the Quantum Moon

Being a Quantum Object, the rule of observing a Quantum Object found on Giant's Deep applies to this object as well:

Viewing an Image of a Quantum object and the object itself are the same thing.

With this knowledge we can land on the Quantum Moon. Once you spot it on the horizon or in the shadow of another planet, head towards it.

If you're having trouble spotting it, spin in circles in your ship looking for a dark small planet with a white halo circling one of the other planets in the solar system. It moves when you're not looking at it so every time you spin, it will move locations. Eventually you should be able to spot it.

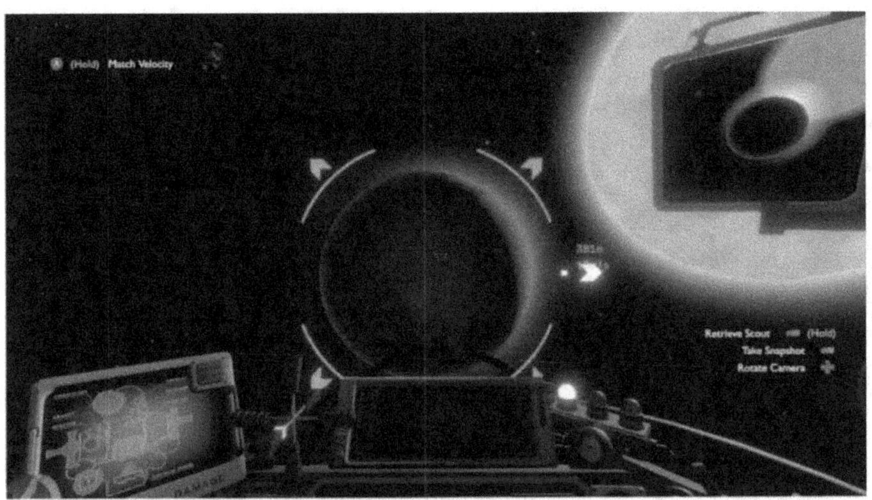

While still in your ship and with it positioned in front of you, fire your scout ahead to take a photo of the moon and keep that photo up on your dashboard as you approach. Thankfully with this photo up, you can now land on the Quantum Moon. It can be slightly more tricky than landing on other locations, as you won't be able to use your landing camera, as this counts as looking away from the Moon, and it will move.

Getting to the Sixth Location

Once you land on the planet, you'll find yourself consistently on the South Pole of the planet. This is part of the mystery of this place. And you may remember the rule of the Tower of Quantum Knowledge that you must be on the North Pole to travel to the 6th location.

In this area you should spot a large Nomai Tower with Quantum mechanics applied to it. If you don't initially spot it, again spin around until it appears.

Head on up to it, and open the door to go inside. Inside you should see a visual of what planet you find yourself on along with images of each planet in the solar system and a switch that controls the lights within the tower. On the opposite wall you'll also find Nomai writings reminding you to remember the three Quantum Rules:

Viewing an Image of a Quantum object and the object itself are the same thing. (You used this to get here so you won't need it again in the riddle)

If in contact with a quantum object and in total darkness, you will travel with that quantum object.

To reach the sixth location, the tower must be on the North Pole.

We are about to solve this puzzle for you, so if you want to figure it out yourself, read no further.

To get to the sixth location, we need to move the Tower to the North Pole of whatever planet it lies on. Closing the door of the Tower and switching the lights off teleports the tower to different locations as evidenced by the moving locator on the wall. We'll need to incrementally move the tower North. To do so, turn the lights off and move locations, then head outside. If you're able to move north, you've made progress. Once you hit a wall, spin around and look for the tower once again. Enter and repeat the process until you are on a planet where you can continue north. Which planet allows you to head north is random, so you'll need to experiment within your own game.

Eventually you'll find yourself able to access the North Pole of one of your locations. Allow the tower to enter into the space of the north pole by spinning around and enter it.

Now with the tower on the North Pole, you can turn the lights off and on, until you find the locator on the Sixth Location indicator. Once you've done this, congratulations! You've made the pilgrimage to the sixth location. Step outside and meet a new comrade.

The Sixth Location

Arriving at the Sixth Location, you'll find yourself at the North Pole. Now that you spent all that time arriving at the North Pole it's time to head to its Southern counterpart. Make your way down to the South Pole, where you'll find (SURPRISE!) a NOMAI!

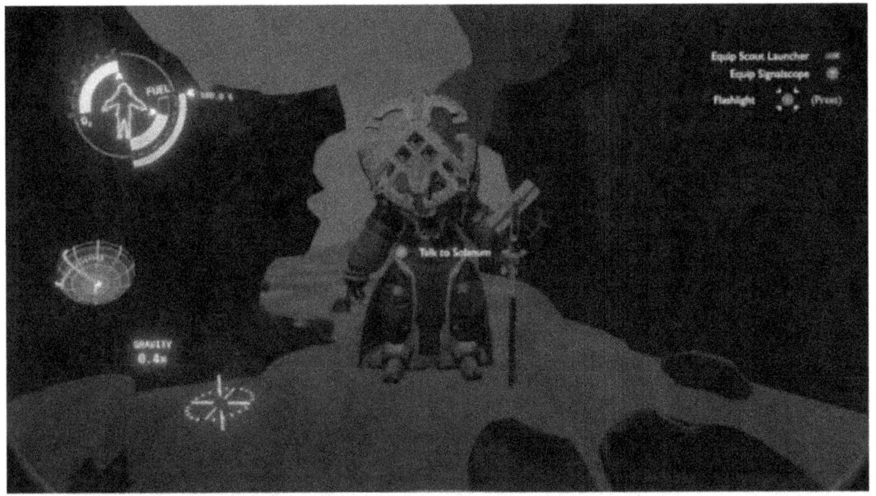

This is Solanum. But unfortunately he doesn't speak your language. Though you do have your translator, so when you ask who he is, he displays several stones with images on them to help you communicate.

There's symbols for the verbs "Explain" and "Identify" and you can combine these with the symbols for "Me," "Quantum Moon," "You," and "Eye of the Universe."

Combining these symbols on the two columns laid out in front of Solanum, he'll write text on the wall to his left that you can then decipher with your translator.

You learn several things from Solanum:

The Quantum Moon was sacred to the Nomai as the closest they could get to the Eye of the Universe.

The Quantum Moon is the Eye of the Universe's Moon, and the two share characteristics, making the Eye quantum as well.

The strange happenings of Quantum Shards and the Quantum moon rise exponentially as you approach the Eye of the Universe (prepare for some strange stuff to happen should you ever arrive there).

HOW TO BEAT OUTER WILDS

How to Obtain the Advanced Warp Core

First up is obtaining the Advanced Warp Core needed to power the Vessel and transport you to the Eye. Once you wake up on Timber Hearth, hop in your ship and beeline it to Ash Twin. Land your ship on one of the poles so that it doesn't get beamed up to Ember Twin via the sandstorm connecting the planets.

As you probably know by now, Ash Twin houses warp stations to all the other planets on its surface, revealed as the sands are pulled away. This is known as the Ash Twin Project, and uses a massive amount of power housed at the core of the planet to make it all run. Even though we're not trying to get to another planet, but instead the center of this one, some of the process remains the same.

Firstly, you'll need to find the buildings housing the warp stations for Ember Twin and Ash Twin. These will appear in order of the solar system, with the Sun Station building being revealed first, followed by the Twins' towers. The Ash Twin tower is represented by a broken building while the whole building next to it is Ember Twin. We'll be working with the Ash Twin tower.

Wait for the sands to pull away, revealing a bridge that ties the two buildings together, then park yourself under this bridge and wait.

Eventually the sands will reveal a doorway into the Ash Twin building, with a dead Nomai in front of it.

Once this is revealed, wait until the sand tornado makes its way around and then walk into the room while in the center of the sandstorm. After doing so, you'll be teleported into the center of Ash Twin, where the whole operation is powered.

Here you can find lots of information to translate and learn from, so if you wish to take the time to do this, you can probably count on having to repeat your cycle to fully complete the steps on this page. As a quick recap, you can discover that the information housed from the memory statues is stored here, and along the wall, Nomai have written testimonials of all their contributions to the parts of the projects they've worked on. You also learn that because of the failure of the sun station, they had talked about how the sun coming to its natural conclusion would also trigger the cycle, which is where our own story began. Neat.

Heading past all the translatable text, you'll find two switches you'll need to trigger to get the Advanced Warp Core. The first switch you'll find is a large ball on the floor. Move it along its path and up the tube in front of you to open the hatch above you containing the Warp Core.

Next, further ahead, you'll find a switch to turn off the gravity of the whole room. Doing so, you can then boost up to the Advanced Warp Core and remove it from the housing.

Once you remove the housing, when you die, without power for the system feeding memories to you in the past, you won't reset as you have before, instead seeing a "You Died" screen. Thankfully, this doesn't matter to your progress as you wake up from the beginning of that day.

Once you have the Warp Core in hand, make your way to the warp station you came in from, and looking down, you'll be teleported out of the core and back to the Ash Twin Tower. Then, head to your ship and make your way towards Dark Bramble.

How to Get to the Vessel

Hopefully, you've already taken the time to find the 3rd Escape Pod and made your way to the Vessel already found within Dark Bramble, so now you can simply retrace your method to return.

However, if you haven't yet explored that, here's a shortcut of the steps necessary to get to the Vessel:

Tune your signal scope to "Distress Signal" (Find a Distress Signal from the Escape Pod on Brittle Hollow or Ember Twin to gain the ability to do this)

Follow the Distress Signal found on Dark Bramble

Head into Dark Bramble and continue following the point of light that is the Distress Signal, using only one tic of boost to avoid detection from the Anglerfish there.

Head into the second seed and continue following the Distress Signal until you reach the 3rd Escape Pod.

Follow the cubes of light until you reach the small seed with the floating Nomai corpses around it.

Fire your Scout into the seed, revealing the Vessel's location in the seed within the orange light.

Follow the signal source and head into the third seed.

DON'T MOVE AS YOU PASS THE THREE ANGLERFISH.

Once the 3 Anglerfish are in the fog behind you slowly boost toward the final seed, and you'll come out the other side in front of the Vessel.

How to Get to the Eye of the Universe

Once you've made it to the Vessel, you're nearly there if you have the Advanced Warp Core and the coordinates.

Land on the platform near the Vessel and exit your ship. Head toward the hole to the right of the platform blasted into the side of the ship, and head down the hallway found there. On your left, you'll find the control room for the ship.

Once here, you should see a spot to place the warp core directly ahead of you. Float towards it and place the Advanced Warp Core in the slot.

This will trigger the artificial gravity of the ship, allowing you to more easily move around and solve the puzzle coming up.

You'll find a switch on the floor with a ball you can move. You'll want to take the ball and move it to the right counterclockwise around the pillar. This will reveal a hexagonal panel at the front of the ship.

If you've discovered the coordinates to the Eye of the Universe at the core of Giant's Deep, as you approach this station, they should pop up in the bottom left corner of your screen. You'll now be entering in the coordinates into the machine, using the ball as an input device. Carefully maneuver the ball into each shape, then bring it to the bottom of the panel and drag it to the right to rotate it to the next side.

If you make a mistake on a panel, simply drag the ball back over the incorrect input to remove it, or drag the ball all the way left along the bottom to rotate the pillar the opposite way.

Below you can see the solutions to the three coordinates:

Panel 1:

Panel 2:

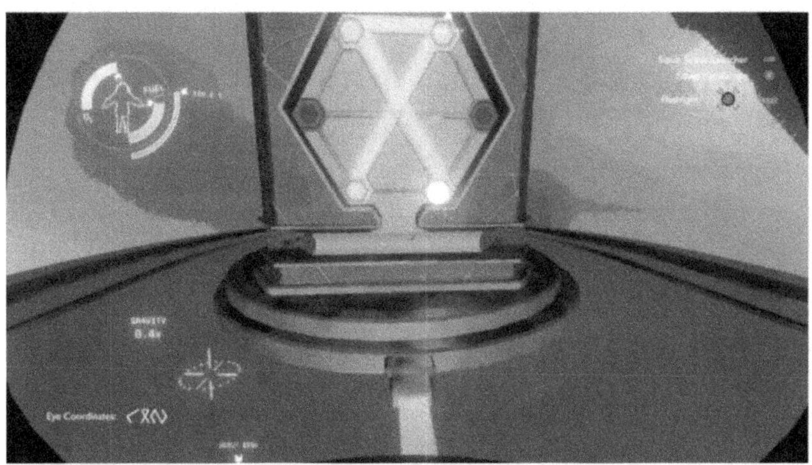

Panel 3:

After imputing these coordinates, the device will lower into the ground. Now you may think you need to drag the ball back clockwise around the pillar and use the switch near the entrance. Doing so will create a warp point. However, this warp point only brings you back outside the ship on Dark Bramble.

Instead once the device lowers, simply use the switch there, moving it up to unlock a warp that takes you to the Eye of the Universe.

Eye of the Universe

Now at the Eye of the Universe, everything seems dark and it can be hard to figure out what to do next. We can now use the second switch we mentioned earlier. Head back to the ball that goes around the pillar in the center of the room. Move it clockwise around the pillar, creating a black hole that you can use to exit the Vessel.

Entering it, you'll find yourself outside the Vessel on the North Pole of the Eye. Make your way south, watching all the oddities of the planet unfold before you.

Reaching the South Pole, you'll find a large fractured dome you can enter and use the walls of to climb upside down. Once a the top of the dome, jump off into the black hole void below.

Falling into it, you'll find yourself in the original building with the statue found on Timber Hearth. Exploring around, it looks as if this is this building years in the future, with your people knowing you found the Eye of the Universe. Curious.

Make your way upstairs climbing the ramp spiraling around the center of the room. On a small platform in the center of the second floor, you'll see a representation of millions of lights with the prompt "Observe."

Doing so, you'll pan out of the building and the planet to see the whole of the universe, and as it pans out into thousands of tiny lights, the space shifts, and those lights become lanterns in a vast forest of trees.

Eventually all the lights flicker out, and an unidentified signal will be found nearby. Use your signalscope to track down a tree found in the darkness. Use your knowledge of quantum objects on this tree, spinning around until the tree becomes the kindling for a campfire you can light.

Continue spinning and a chair will appear next to the fire, and then Esker will appear.

Using your signalscope, you can begin to track down the other frequencies found within the space.

Inside a broken and crumbling building, you'll find a Banjo allowing Riebeck to return to the campfire.

On a tree stump surrounded by tiny orange jellyfish, you'll find a harmonica, allowing Feldspar to return.

Finding a large telescope looking out at red stars of light, you can use your signalscope and zoom in on a floating drum set to gather, allowing Chert to return.

Following the pointing directional signs of the poem found on Timber Hearth, you'll find a hammock in the trees with a trumpet you can gather to return Gabbro to the campfire.

Finally, if you spoke with Solanum at the 6th location, you should find a signal of the skeletons of some Nomai all pointing upward. Using quantum rules you can get these skeletons to stack on top of one another, which when they do so reveals a Nomai spacecraft. Use the beam to travel upward into the craft. Then, use the control panel and move the switch into the leftmost option. You'll rush forward into a ray of light, and can gather the mask of a Nomai, which will cause Solanum to appear by the fire.

After all of the travelers have appeared around the campfire, speak with each to get them to begin playing a lovely tune in sync with one another. Doing so a large smoky orb will appear in the sky above the campfire.

Jumping into it, you'll trigger a cutscene of a gigantic explosion, along with the end credits.

Post Credits

After the credits role, you'll see a short cutscene of a universe mirroring that of the title screen you see when you open the game, with a campfire and campers beneath the stars.

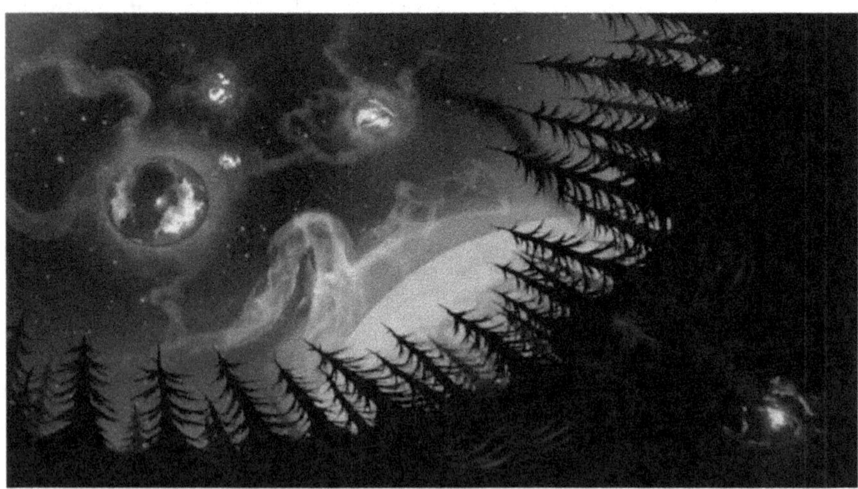

This most likely alludes to the fact that while you may not have saved the your species and the end of all life for you and your comrades, Life carried on and became something completely new.

Congratulations on completion of the game. Did you find everything within it? If not, make sure to visit each page to uncover everything to be found in Outer Wilds.

HOW TO START ECHOES OF THE EYE DLC

Echoes of the Eye is Outer Wilds' first and only DLC, and just like the rest of the game, delving into this game update isn't exactly straightforward. Starting Echoes of the Eye is a bit of a puzzle. In this guide, you'll learn the secret to accessing the DLC.

Timber Hearth Museum Exhibit

To get started, visit the new exhibit at the Timber Hearth observatory and museum. It's just to the left of the entrance. The plaque describes a project that makes it possible for all explorers to have a handy galaxy map. It's time to head to the radio tower to learn more about the deep space satellite.

Make sure you have the launch codes before leaving the observatory. You'll need your ship.

Timber Hearth Radio Tower

The easiest way to get to the radio tower is by hopping in your ship and flying straight over. It's northeast of Timber Hearth's village. If you feel lost, follow the river then keep going east. You'll see a small patch of trees and the radio tower.

Land at the radio tower and hop out. No need to worry about your suit for now. You won't be doing any major jumping.

Enter the small grove of trees across the radio tower. Here you'll find an unlit campfire (that you can light if you wish) and a note on how to dose off. This will allow you to pass time at campfires without completing resetting the day.

Solving the Radio Tower Puzzle

Now, enter the radio tower. This is where you'll find your "real" (meaning obscure) instructions for what to do next.

The radio tower is a small building. Each of its walls has four photos and in the center of the main room is an audio log about the deep space satellite. There's something wrong about one of the photos. Here's a quick hint before we outright give the solution to this first puzzle: What's different between each of the photos? Consider counting the objects you see in each.

The answer lies in their differences. The answer isn't Gabbro, of course. He was sent after this issue occurred.

Here's what doesn't belong: in Satellite Angle: 40 degrees, there's a circular spot over the sun. Excluding the sun, there should only be six celestial items in each photo.

Gabbro goes on to inspect the satellite when it's at position 137 degrees and finds nothing wrong with it. That means you need to get to the Satellite when it's at 40 degrees.

How to Get to the Echoes of the Eye DLC Area

If you've been playing a while already, it's worth resetting your loop to make this next part as easy as possible and to give yourself as much time as possible in the next area. The sun is still dying, after all.

To start the true Echoes of the Eye DLC, you'll need to get to the Deep Space Satellite before it gets too far past 40 degrees. It moves slow, but it's in your best interest if you move quickly. You can try to make your way to this position on your own after the satellite is moved past, but it's unnecessarily difficult to do so.

You'll know you still have time to make it to the deep space satellite if you can't access your galaxy map! You can test it by pressing tab or the left window or menu button on a controller.

Track the satellite and fly to it while it's above the galaxy. As you stay with the satellite, you should start to notice something appearing over the sun. Once you see the black spot, fly toward it.

As you get close you should notice the sun starting to disappear.

Then, the sun will disappear entirely. The rest is up to you.

HOW TO RETURN TO THE ECHOES OF THE EYE DLC

The end of the galaxy comes for us all at some point, and the same remains true in Outer Wilds' Echoes of the Eye DLC. Fret not, you won't have to track the deep space satellite to get back to the DLC area. Here's how to get back to the strange new location.

How to Get Back to The Stranger

Gone are your days of hunting that satellite. Now, you can simply track the location of the DLC area from your Ship Log and fly to it at any time.

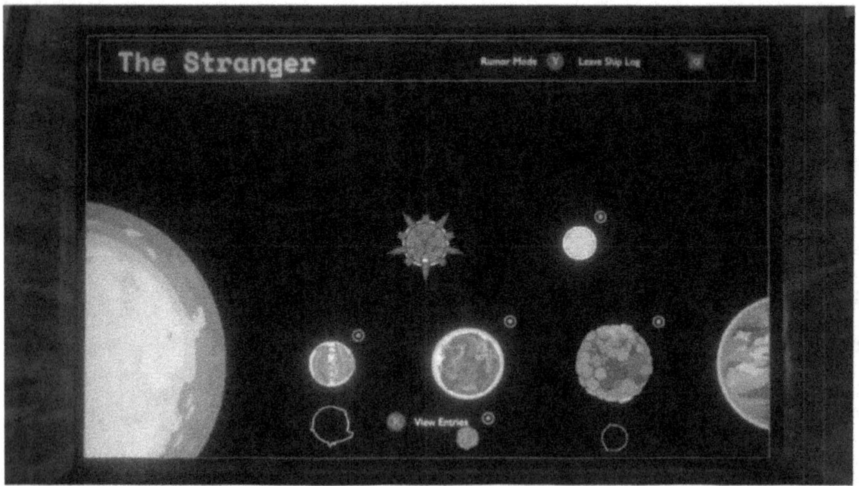

Select "The Stranger" in the Ship Log. Then, once in The Stranger's menu, you can add the HUD marker and track its location. You can autopilot your way to The Stranger, but you may need to give your ship a little nudge to actually enter the vessel.

Upon returning, you won't need to fly toward the sun either. You'll see the exterior of The Stranger and can enter directly. You can leave too! Just be careful not to bang up your ship as you enter or exit.

ECHOES OF THE EYE ENDINGS GUIDE

Ending Option 1

Once you've obtained your Advanced Warp Core, board your ship and fly to "The Stranger".

After landing aboard the mysterious vessel and entering one of its many areas you can do just about anything you want as you wait for the sun to explode. Just make sure that when it does explode that you're in The Stranger and holding the Warp Core.

If you want to reach the ending quicker feel free to approach any of the green-flamed braziers in The Stranger to "Doze Off" and fast-forward time. Just remember that each of the Outer Wilds' loops is 22-minutes in length so make sure not to oversleep and miss the end of the world.

Because The Stranger moves out of the sun's blast radius you will survive the explosion. A title card will appear explaining that you are the lone survivor before fading to black and rolling the game's credits.

Ending Option 2

After obtaining the Advanced Warp Core fly your ship back to The Stranger. With your Warp Core in hand, find an artifact in either the "River Lowlands", "Hidden Gorge", or "Damaged Laboratory". Trade the Warp Core for the artifact, leaving the Warp Core behind.

Now that you have an artifact, take it to any of the "Ritual Rooms" or the "Reservoir". Ritual Rooms can be found in the River Lowlands, Cinder Isles, and Hidden Gorge. To locate the Ritual Rooms within these areas, find the corresponding building that has a green circle on its exterior.

Then once inside you'll see several murals. Find the mural with a Saturn-like ringed planet and move the lanterns in front of the mural so it goes dark. This will reveal a hidden path to one of the Ritual Rooms.

Meanwhile, if you intend to travel to the Reservoir with your artifact then you need to enter the Submerged Structure as described on the

Reservoir page.

The Submerged Structure and all three Ritual Rooms will house a brazier with a bright green flame. Stand on the flame until you die.

This will teleport you to The Secret World. Shortly after entering The Secret World a title card will appear before fading to black and rolling the credits.

True Ending

The true ending to Outer Wilds: Echoes of the Eye DLC includes many of the steps needed to get to the "Eye of the Universe" ending in the main game.

Again, a guide for this ending can be found on the How to Beat Outer Wilds page.

However, in order to get the DLC's true ending, you must also open the "Sealed Vault" on The Stranger to free "The Prisoner". After freeing them they will leave their Vision Torch in the ground. Walk into the torch's glowing light to see a vision of The Prisoner joining you.

If you fail to do this prior to trying to achieve the DLC's true ending you will instead get the main game's "Eye of the Universe" ending.

Follow the steps in the Eye of the Universe page and this guide will begin after you have jumped into the black hole and returned to Timber Hearth.

When you land in Timber Hearth you should notice that you're now years into the future and that your people are aware that you found the Eye of the Universe.

You can explore the area and read the many plaques on display including the plaque in front of the Timber Hearth radio tower that you visited when first starting your playthrough of the DLC.

Next, make your way upstairs. On the second floor, walk up to the lights and "Observe" them. The lights will then transition into lanterns in a forest.

Use your "signalscope" to identify a small reddish tree surrounded by stones. Spin around and the tree will become a campfire that you can light. Continue spinning and Esker will appear by the fire.

Your signalscope will serve as your guide as you hunt down various frequencies in the area that lead to instruments corresponding to all of the individuals you've met on your journey.

The number of instruments and individuals present in the area will be dependent on your previous gameplay and how many sections of Outer Wilds you have completed.

Once you find a character's instrument they will be summoned by the campfire where they'll wait for you.

After you find The Prisoner's instrument they will stand a few feet away from the campfire. They will ask to join the campfire if you speak to them. Accept and they will join the others with their instrument.

The Prisoner - Instrument can be found in an underground area after you extinguish all of the candles within.

Gabbro - Trumpet can be found in a hammock amongst the trees.

Feldspar- Harmonica can be found on a tree stump surrounded by orange jellyfish.

Riebeck - Banjo can be found inside a ruined building.

Chert - Drum can be found by using a telescope to find it floating near amongst red stars

Solanum - If you spoke to Solanum, she can be summoned to the campfire by finding the signal of Nomai skeletons pointing upward. Stack these skeletons on top of each other by using what you've learned about "quantum rules". A Nomai spacecraft will then be revealed. Use the tractor beam to enter the craft. Gather the mask of a Nomai to summon Solanum to the campfire.

Speak to every character surrounding the campfire and inform them that you are ready. They'll begin playing their instruments in unison and conjure an orb above the campfire.

After they stop playing the forest goes dark. Talk to all of the characters if this is your first time completing the Outer Wilds. Each character will say the same thing they did in the main game's ending except of course for the newly added Prisoner.

The Prisoner says, "...How beautiful. It's different than I'd envisioned. Whatever happens next, I do not think it is to be feared".

When you're ready to progress jump into the orb to cause an explosion and the credits will roll.

If you wait out the credits you'll be rewarded with a post-credit scene. A title card will read, "14.3 Billion Years Later", before showing you a beautiful galactic image with campers around a fire underneath.

Congratulations, you have now completed the Outer Wilds DLC, Echoes of the Eye. If you would like to explore more of the Outer Wilds, continue reading through the many guides for both the DLC and the main title.

ABOUT THE AUTHOR

I When I finding new tricks, tips, and strategies to beat each other, they came up with a brilliant idea. Let's take these hours of gaming expertise, and share these skills with like mind people. At that moment, the Outer Wilds Complete Guide were born. With more exciting gaming books being developed in the Lab as we speak. I am creating a buzz in the gaming guide publishing world, with a ground swell of followers, anxiously awaiting my new releases.